The NEW Fun Encyclopedia

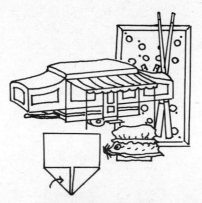

The NEW Fun Encyclopedia

Volume 3 Home and Family Fun

E. O. Harbin
revised by
Bob Sessoms

ABINGDON PRESS

Nashville

THE NEW FUN ENCYCLOPEDIA

VOLUME III. HOME AND FAMILY FUN

Library of Congress Cataloging in Publication Data

(revised for vol. 3)
HARBIN, E. O. (Elvin Oscar), 1885–
　The new fun encyclopedia.
　Rev. ed. of: The fun encyclopedia. © 1940.
　Bibliography: v. 1, p. Includes index.
　Contents: v. 1. Games— v. 3. Home and family fun.
　1. Amusements—Collected works. 2. Games—Collected works. 3. Entertaining—Collected works. I. Sessoms, Bob. II. Harbin, E. O. (Elvin Oscar), 1885–1955. Fun encyclopedia. III. Title
GV1201.H383 1983 　　　794 　　　83-2818

ISBN 0-687-27756-6 (v. 3)

0-687-27754-X (v. 1)
0-687-27755-8 (v. 2)
0-687-27757-4 (v. 4)
0-687-27758-2 (v. 5)
0-687-27759-0 (set)

MANUFACTURED BY THE PARTHENON PRESS AT NASHVILLE, TENNESSEE, UNITED STATES OF AMERICA

CONTENTS

INTRODUCTION

*I*n the original *Fun Encyclopedia*, E. O. Harbin, in his creative manner, stated the age-old axiom, "The family that plays together will be more likely to stay together." And he included a poem that is as relevant today as it was more than forty years ago:

> "Home, sweet home," the poet sang
> In days that were of old,
> But now the home has just become
> A parking place, I'm told;
> We park to eat, a bit to sleep,
> And then we're on the run—
> The office, movies, clubs, and dates;
> No time for family fun!

It is true that we are on the go constantly and have very little opportunity for any time at home, much less quality time. Today's parent is primarily a carpool chaffeur or an errand taxi driver. With ballgames, piano and dance lessons, church and school activities, there is little time for the family to be together as a unit. So each family must decide for itself to prioritize the activities any individual member can engage in, in order to protect all members of the family. Time must be set aside to be together.

The New Fun Encyclopedia attempts to provide ideas for getting the family back together again. This book does not have all the answers, but I hope it will be a catalyst to start things moving in the right direction. There are many single-parent families today, and care must be taken, too, to keep these units from being destroyed.

Space does not permit, nor is it the intention of this volume to be a sounding board for "what ails America," or to determine the reason for the deterioration of the family unit. The bibliography provides a list of books that deal with the family and suggest ways families can fulfill the major purpose for which God designed them. The intention of this volume is to offer guidance and ideas, so that family members can become involved with one another once more. It is not too late! And it is worth trying for!

So, family, begin to play together, and you will more than likely stay together. But don't forget the other saying: "Families that pray together stay together." Here's hoping you have a family full of fun.

Thank you, Carolyn, who guided our family in choosing quality time. And Robin, Jami, and Jon, who kept it fun.

BOB SESSOMS

1

FAMILY NIGHTS AT HOME

The family night at home is not a new idea, but one that should be revived. In the last century the home was the center of activity, worship, education, and work. In today's society, however, we do not see many families doing things together. There is a lack of communication between parents and children, husband and wife, brother and sister. Even the method inherent in the word *communication* has changed. At one time the family was considered the center of communication in the home, but the television set now seems to hold that place. It has driven a wedge between family members; now they just sit and watch. Very little interaction or old-fashioned conversation takes place in the home today.

This volume is an attempt to help families to return to communication—to communicate values or just get to know one another, just be a family. To be a family is to be together—sharing, loving, playing, praying, telling, listening, talking, walking, experiencing, laughing, crying, hugging, touching, respecting, caring, working, understanding, kissing, forgiving, hurting, healing, encouraging, believing, disciplining, smiling, communicating—*together*.

Family nights will enable families to enjoy time together. And this time together must be a priority time—nothing short of an emergency should interfere. Whether a family stays at home or goes out together, each member must make every effort to take part in the family activity.

The ideas offered here are only suggestions, springboards from which your family can create its own activities. Remember that there should be a point to each night's activity. So plan with a purpose—even if the purpose is just to have fun!

A Form to Follow: Have a family council. Explain that you are setting aside one night a week (or a month) to be together. Nothing is to interfere with the schedule. This must be agreed upon by the entire family. Every member must pledge loyalty to this special time.

Ask the family to brainstorm. List all the ideas you can come up with for Family Nights at Home, then prioritize them from most important to least important. With a calendar, plan those activities your family decides upon. You might even suggest a menu for the meal for a particular night's activity.

All family nights should have a similar format. The evening should begin with the meal. Each member of your family who is able should help with the preparation of the food and with the clean-up. The table should be cleared and the dishes done and put away before the activity begins, although sometimes it is best to save dessert until after the activity.

Vary the menu from Sloppy Joes to a full-course meal; from pizza to prime rib; from soup and salad to turkey with all the fixings. And vary your dress accordingly, from casual to Sunday best. This is a special time—prepare for it.

FAMILY FOTO NIGHT

What is more enjoyable than bringing out the old photo album, the boxes full of old photographs, the countless slides, and even the old movies (if you have any), and going back in time to relive the good old days. But if your family is like most, your photographs are not in an album, nor are the slides in order, much less in a tray. Take tonight and get it all together.

Purchase what you need: several photograph albums, filler pages, glue or photo corners, trays for the slides, and whatever else you will need. Divide the family into two groups, one for photographs and one for slides. The photo group should first sort the photographs, either chronologically or into categories such as baby pictures, family pictures, individual pictures, vacation pictures, and so on. If possible, a brief description should be written under or on the back of each photograph as it is placed in the album. The group working on slides should try to get them in order by month, year, and number (1, 2, 3, etc.). Most slides were taken in progression and should remain as taken for chronological significance.

After all this has been accomplished, everyone can sit down and look at the photograph albums. While the slides are being viewed, serve a favorite dessert.

SUPER STAR NIGHT

We are familiar with the super-star competition. Why not have one at home? Select games that are educational, or teach games that were meaningful to you as a youngster. On a piece of poster board, list the games and the number of points that may be scored for each one.

You may schedule either active games or inactive games or some of each. Suggestions:

Hangman—A player has a word in mind and puts down as many dashes as there are letters in the word. A letter is called. If the word contains that letter, the writer must put the letter in each space where it appears in the word. If the guess is wrong, the writer begins to draw the scaffold suggested in the diagram. At each wrong guess, the writer draws more of the scaffold, beginning with line 1 and continuing with line 2, 3, and so on. The object is to hang the whole man. Eyes, nose, and mouth may be added, if desired. A skillful player usually calls the vowels first. Some difficult words are *sylph, tryst, way,* and *wax.* With a large crowd, divide into teams and use chalkboards. One team chooses a word and tries to hang the other team. Any player can call a letter.

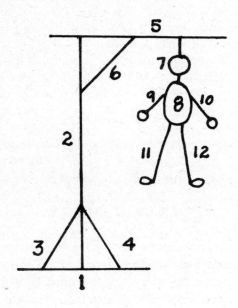

Pie Pan Roll—Each player gets one turn to roll a pie pan from a starting line. Mark the spot where the pan lands with tape bearing the player's name.

Muffin Tin Toss—Each player attempts to toss ten small washers, one at a time, into a muffin tin. The player who lands the most is declared winner.

Tit-Tat-Toe—Two players. One player chooses X, the other, O. The players take turns placing Xs and Os in the spaces. The player who succeeds in placing three Xs or Os in a row wins. May be used as a team game, with players marking on a chalkboard.

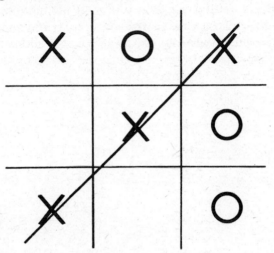

Indoor Shot Put—Players stand behind a line and attempt to toss a cotton ball as far as possible. Each player gets one try. Place a piece of tape with the player's name on it at the point where the cotton ball lands.

Javelin Straw Toss—Each player tosses an ordinary drinking straw for distance. A tape bearing the player's name is placed where the straw lands.

Potato Roll—Players are timed as they crawl around an obstacle course of chairs, pushing potatoes with their noses.

Ball Bounce—Players *bounce* a tennis ball into a trash can set five or ten feet away. Each player is allowed five bounces. A point for each successful basket.

Making Squares—This is a good game for two people, but a family can play it by taking turns. Make five or more rows of dots. Players take turns connecting any two dots with a straight line, except diagonally. Whenever a player can finish a square by adding a line, that player's initial is placed in the enclosed space. When all dots have been connected, the players' scores are indicated by the number of squares bearing their initials.

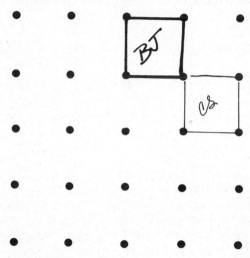

Awards Ceremony—After the completion of competition, total the scores and make awards: paper cups with the names of the players written in felt-tip marker. Be sure everyone receives something, perhaps a card with such titles as:

> Best Sport of Our Super-Star Night
> Tried Hardest in Our Super-Star Night.

Make this night fun for the whole family. Boast about how well everyone did. Emphasize that although winning is the goal of a game, it is more important to do your very best, no matter what the outcome. For dessert, serve the family's favorite pudding.

WE LOVE YOU NIGHT

Everyone needs affirmation; everyone needs to be loved. Each member of a family needs this every day. It doesn't hurt to have a time set aside for affirming one another, so have a We Love You Night. Prepare the meal everyone seems to like best. After the meal is finished and the table cleared (and dishes done), return to the table for this game.

What Is Love?—Give each family member a pencil and a copy of the following word puzzle. The puzzle contains words about love, written vertically, horizontally, or backward. Find and circle the words listed under the puzzle. Then discuss the meaning of the words. Add to the list, and read First Corinthians 13:4-8 (answers on p. 16).

```
E  Y  A  L  I  S  T  E  N  I  N  G  G
N  B  Q  G  N  I  S  S  I  K  B  X  N
C  A  R  I  N  G  U  Z  J  I  E  K  I
O  B  V  N  W  U  R  F  T  N  L  T  H
U  N  D  E  R  S  T  A  N  D  I  N  G
R  X  J  V  E  H  O  M  E  E  E  E  U
A  T  G  I  S  A  U  I  Z  M  V  I  A
G  O  D  G  P  R  C  L  X  N  I  T  L
I  C  B  R  E  E  H  Y  V  L  N  A  A
N  S  K  O  C  S  M  I  L  E  G  P  D
G  U  H  F  T  R  O  P  P  U  S  K  F
J  G  H  E  N  I  L  P  I  C  S  I  D
```

Answers:

BABY	KISSING
BELIEVING	LAUGHING
CARING	LISTENING
ENCOURAGING	PATIENT
DISCIPLINE	RESPECT
FAMILY	SHARE
FORGIVEN	SMILE
GOD	SUPPORT
HOME	TOUCH
HUG	UNDERSTANDING
KIND	

Make Love Notes—With construction paper, felt-tip markers, crayons, glue, and scissors, let each person design and construct cards with expressions of love for all the other members of the family. When all the cards are completed, have each person in turn sit at the head of the table while the others present their cards. Each honoree must read the cards out loud so that the whole family has this chance to hear how everyone feels about the others. Then let everyone make cards with similar expressions for the grandparents. Mail these with long letters written by all the family.

Then bring on the dessert for everyone to enjoy. Share your feelings about the evening. It would be nice to hug one another and say, "I love you!"

FAMILY HOBBY AND CRAFT NIGHT

This night is just what the title says—a night for hobbies and crafts. Many children collect things, as do adults. Let each family member bring a collection or hobby to share with the rest of the family.

After sharing, involve the family in a craft. You might hold this fun night several times a year. Here are a few quickie crafts to use.

Toy Indian Drum—Collect #10 cans from a restaurant or church kitchen. Clean the cans thoroughly and cut out both ends with a can opener. Cut 2 pieces of inner tubing, leather, or heavy vinyl material four inches larger than the can's diameter for the top and bottom of each drum. With a leather punch or other sharp pointed object, punch holes about one inch from the edge and two inches apart, all around the sides of the material. With twine, lace two pieces to each can, alternating between top and bottom circles. Decorate the material with felt-tip markers.

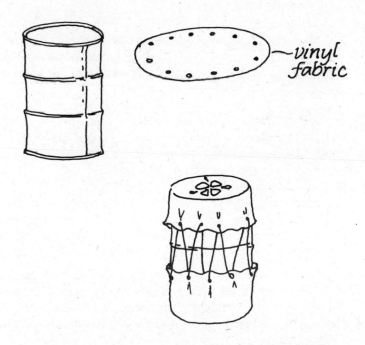

—*vinyl fabric*

Rock Images—Have on hand several small smooth rocks, epoxy glue, acrylic paints, brushes, and "wiggle eyes." Let each family member create something with a rock or rocks—figures of animals, people, or objects (cars, planes, etc.), gluing rocks together if necessary. After the glue has dried, paint your creations. These can be used for paper weights, gifts, or they can just be keepsakes. Be sure to clean the paintbrushes afterward.

Nature Prints—For this project you will need onionskin paper, colored chalk or crayon, various flat objects from nature (leaves, rocks, tree bark), and hair spray or an art fixative.

Let each child choose an object to work with. Lay the paper on the object and, with the chalk or crayon, rub hard enough to make an imprint on the paper. Spray the print to keep it from smearing.

Paper-bag Puppets—Get paper bags the right size to fit over the hand of a child. With felt-tip marker or crayons, children can create their own puppets and give a puppet show.

Animal Masks—This would be a good project for the Halloween season. With large paper bags, children can make their own masks, using felt-tip markers or crayons to create monsters or other characters.

Bookmarks—As gifts for friends, family, or shut-ins, make bookmarks. At a printing office, ask for scrap cuttings or pieces of thick paper about 2 X 5 inches. These bookmarks can be decorated in several ways:

Splatter Paint: You will need either a toothbrush, a piece of metal screen, and paint, or a can of spray paint. Cut out a design (butterfly, flower, bird, leaf, etc.), lay it on the bookmark, and spray paint or splatter paint. Allow to dry before using.

Potato Print: Slice a potato in half. With a plastic knife or a spoon, create a print design by cutting away parts of the potato so that what remains forms a picture, a face, or an object. Using a paint roller and tempera paint, roll the paint over the design. Carefully press the potato onto the bookmark, remove carefully, and allow to dry.

This project not only involves making something for someone else, but also teaches family members a skill. And in the process, everyone has fun.

YARD NIGHT (OR DAY)

An activity for spring gets the family out into the yard. Give assignments to every family member. Someone might pick up the trash that has accumulated during the winter months; someone might rake the leaves left from fall; older children or adults might till the garden; others might trim the shrubs or trees. This is a time for all to chip in and do whatever needs to be done to get the yard ready for spring.

A time for planting can be included. Bulbs, tomato plants, other plants or seeds, and new shrubs or trees could be ceremonially planted. Even a bird house might be erected. With everyone helping, when the seeds begin to sprout and the plants begin to bear flowers or fruit, every family member will have a part in rejoicing.

Have sandwiches, lemonade, and other assorted snacks available to munch on during these hours.

FRONTIER NIGHT

An empty #10 can will be needed for each member of the family (younger children need supervision; preschoolers may watch). Completely remove one end of each can with a can opener. With tin snips, cut a four-inch opening on one side of each can at the bottom (the open end). With another type can opener, punch a hole in each can near the top on the opposite side from the hole, to serve as a chimney. Place each can on level ground.

In a charcoal grill, have coals ready for cooking; carefully place several hot coals under each can; allow time for the cans to heat through. Cut bacon strips in half; fry these on top of the cans. Do not let grease overflow and drip into fire. Gently tear the centers out of pieces of bread. When the bacon is done, remove it and place the outside part of a piece of bread on each can. Break an egg into the hole in each piece of bread. When done on one side, flip over. This makes a good outdoor meal using a different method of cooking.

After the meal, clean up the area and throw away the cans—they can be used only once for this type of cooking. However, one could serve as a stove if a frying pan were used.

A Critter Race—Let each member of the family search the yard and capture some critters (worms, frogs, lizards, beetles, bugs, etc.). Draw a circle in the dirt—or if there is no dirt, on the patio. Divide the critters into categories—grasshoppers, crickets, beetles, and so on. Place the critters in the center of the circle. The first one to cross the line is the winner. After the race, return all the critters to the spots where they were found.

Understanding the Weather—If the sun is still in the sky, teach a few old-time methods of predicting the weather:

A red sky at night is a traveler's delight.

The evening gray, the morning red, will pour rain down on your head.

An evening sky that is rose or red means fair weather is ahead.

A "mackerel" sky (a sky that looks like fish scales) usually means fair weather, though it might bring a few showers.

When smoke rises straight up from a campfire, good weather will continue.

When grass is wet with dew on a summer's night, the next morning will be fair and bright.

A pale yellow sky at sunset foretells a rainy day ahead.

A morning rainbow in the west predicts rain on the way.

When crows perform acrobatics in the air, high winds are near.

All odors become more noticeable shortly before a rain.

If there are crickets in your area, you can tell the temperature by listening and counting. Count the number of chirps in fourteen seconds; add forty. The total gives the temperature.

Storytelling—When it begins to get dark, it is time to tell some exciting stories. Several are included in chapter 2 of this volume—or make up your own!

YOUR FAMILY TREE

How many of you really know much about your family tree? Take time to inform your family members about their roots. It can also be interesting to research the meaning of last names. Public libraries usually have this kind of information.

Write to anyone who might know some of your family history. If someone has an old family Bible or old photographs, have them sent to you, upon your promise of their immediate and safe return.

If your family has resided in the same location for many years, you may find information in county records; there may be a book containing information about your ancestry; or you may be acquainted with older people who knew of your family.

With a felt-tip marker, list the names of the children at the top of a piece of posterboard, then add the names of parents, grandparents, and so on, as far back as you can go. You might also include other relatives—sisters, brothers, cousins. Not only will the family be fascinated by all this, but the research might reveal some romantic figure from the past.

Your family might enjoy making the following craft item. It could consist of only your immediate family, or a larger one could include all the grandparents. (Members who are deceased should also be included.)

Gather different sizes of sticks. Glue them together on a piece of wood or board. On each stick, glue two wiggle eyes (available in craft stores). Underneath, write the names of the family members. Use a small eyelet to hang your Family Tree on the wall.

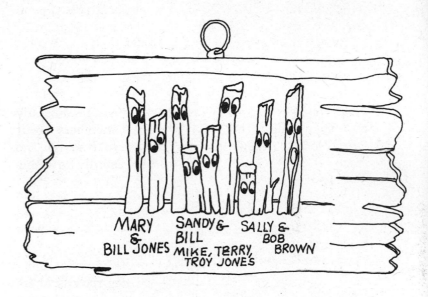

MARY
&
BILL JONES

SANDY &
BILL
MIKE, TERRY,
TROY JONES

SALLY &
BOB
BROWN

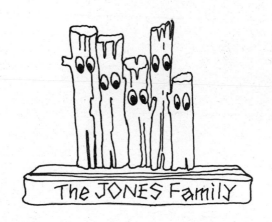

The JONES Family

FAMILY NIGHT UNDER THE STARS

You will need either strong binoculars or a telescope. You could borrow these, or check with leading department stores if you would like to purchase one for the family. This can develop into a fun and educational hobby. You will also need some literature about the stars. Visit the library or a reputable bookstore for this resource. Be certain the book contains charts and diagrams of the constellations.

Before venturing out into the night, review the books and charts. With a sharp pointed instrument, punch holes in the bottom of empty oatmeal boxes to outline the various constellations. By holding a box up to a light, one can readily see the constellation. This makes it easier to locate and identify when you go outside.

Check with the local weather bureau for special heavenly events: a comet, a moon eclipse, the appearance of the Northern Lights.

After stargazing, go inside for refreshments. Or build a campfire—a real one, or light up the grill—and roast hot dogs and marshmallows.

FAMILY NIGHT FIRE DRILL

This is a real opportunity for the family to discuss what to do in case of fire. You might invite a fireman to dinner, to share with the family what you should do in case of fire. If one is not available, go to the fire department and ask for information.

Consider the need for a smoke alarm system. Talk with those who know and purchase the best. Post emergency numbers beside every telephone in the house. Be sure the children know the number to call in case of fire.

Explain to everyone the procedure to follow in case of fire: Be sure everyone is awake. If the house is full of smoke, crawl on hands and knees (not on stomach) to the nearest exit. One of the adults should lead the family in a fire drill to practice leaving the house.

If time permits, some possessions might be saved. Assignments might be made for family members to secure certain items that are easily available. For instance, if all coat hangers in the closets are hooked properly, one can grab an armful of clothes before leaving the house. But possessions are the least important things to save.

Discuss the importance of the right use of fire, the safe use of matches, and the care of fires in the fireplace. This could be a very important family time spent together.

FAMILY FALL FUN FESTIVAL

Halloween is a fun time for children. Instead of going out trick-or-treating, why not have them stay home and have your own fun time? Begin early with a fun menu the entire family participates in. Cook a Halloween stew in an old-fashioned kettle and serve warm corn bread to enhance this meal. After the kitchen has been cleaned up, begin preparing the items for the trick-or-treaters who will be coming to your door.

The family can have popcorn, popcorn balls, and candy apples ready, and make hot chocolate or a favorite fruit punch. As the trick-or-treaters come to the door, greet them wearing scary costumes and invite them in. In the garage, gameroom, or some other room, set up several games. Suggestions: Bean bag toss, dunking for apples, ring toss over chair legs, ball tossed into a bucket, and so on. After the games, serve the refreshments.

If you have the resources, you might take polaroid photos of the youngsters who visit your home.

As much fun as this will be for adults, let your children take charge of the activities.

NOTE: Trick-or-treat activities have been somewhat curtailed in recent years. Many churches, schools, and organizations provide carnivals and other activities as alternatives to the traditional house-to-house visits. One of these could be the answer parents are looking for on Halloween.

FAMILY FIX-IT NIGHT

Before the event, go around the house and search out little items that have been put aside until you could find the "right time" to repair them. Gather the tools needed for each job.

When everything is ready, make assignments compatible to the age and ability of each child. If a job is so difficult that an adult must undertake it, show the children how it is done. This can be a learning time for them.

What needs to be done? Washers need to be replaced on leaky faucets; pictures hung on the wall; furniture moved, dusted, or polished; rugs cleaned; window panes replaced; closets cleaned out; cobwebs removed; bathroom tile cleaned. There are countless repair and cleaning jobs needed in every home. Teach the children how to vacuum, polish, clean, replace a window pane (which they probably broke while playing ball), hammer a nail, and so on.

After everything is "fixed," have some extra-special refreshments ready.

CHRISTMAS FAMILY NIGHTS AT HOME

Christmas is a time to remember the birth of our Savior, Jesus Christ—that is the primary purpose of the holy day. It is also a time for families to reflect on the year past and to share love for one another through the exchange of gifts. Our thoughts during the entire month of December should be focused on the family. Here are some suggestions for a month of Family Nights at Home for Christmas.

Christmas Decorations—There is nothing better than home-created decorations, especially those made by children.

Egg Ornament: Early in the fall, begin to collect whole egg shells. First, remove the contents of the egg. Use a straight pin to make a small hole at one end of the shell, and a larger hole at the other end. Blow in the small hole to force the yolk and white of the egg out the other hole. This can be used for scrambled eggs or in other dishes. Wash the shells out thoroughly to remove any remaining traces of egg and store them carefully.

Several methods may be used to decorate the shells:

Color with Easter-egg coloring.

Glue on figures and designs cut from small-print wrapping paper.

Use felt-tip markers or model paint to create designs.

Spread glue over the shell and roll in glitter.

Glue on photographs of the children taken each year.

The shell may be sprayed with a lacquer-type solution to preserve the decoration. Place a hook in the top to hang it on the tree.

Sweet-Gum-Ball Character: If you have sweet gum trees in your area, gather some sweet-gum balls, leaving the twigs attached. Glue two sweet-gum balls together so that the twig can serve as a nose on a face or as the tail of a creature. With wiggle eyes glued just above the nose (a twig), you will have a special creation. With scraps of felt, cut out a small heart and glue it on the bottom of the sweet-gum ball for feet. Make clothing to dress the creature, if desired. By using imagination, a Santa Claus, a mouse, or a person can be created. Glue a hanger on the top to hang it on the tree.

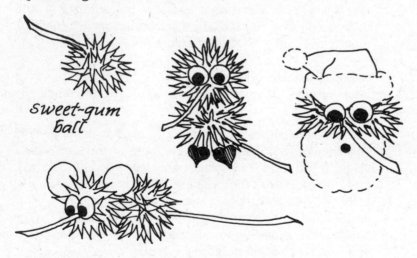

sweet-gum
ball

Bread Dough Ornaments:

4 cups flour	1½ to 1¾ cups cold water
2 cups salt	

Adding water in small amounts, mix the ingredients thoroughly with your fingers until all the dough clings together. Then knead the dough for ten minutes. The consistency should be smooth and elastic.

Roll half the dough into ¼-inch thickness and place on wax paper. Using Christmas cookie cutters, or creating your own design, shape the ornament. With an ice pick, punch a hole in the top for the hanger. Place all ornaments on a greased cookie sheet. Bake in a preheated 350° oven for one hour. Remove and cool.

Use bright acrylic paints to color the ornaments. After the paints have dried, apply four coats of clear spray. Place a string through the hole and add the hanger.

Make Your Own Wreath—Most craft stores have straw or styrofoam wreath shapes available. What you do with the wreath is up to your family's creativity. Suggested materials to place on your wreath: dried flowers, artificial fruit, plastic or live greenery, berries, pine cones, small tree decorations (figures and balls), plastic or cloth ribbons or bows. Various colors of ribbon also may be wrapped around the straw wreath. Calico is popular, in addition to the traditional red and green. You will need a few other supplies: pliable wire (available at most craft stores), pins, wire cutters. Attach the items to the wreath base with the wire. You will need a hook to hang the wreath on the door.

Straw brooms can be decorated in the same way and hung on the door.

Christmas Cards—Cut green or red construction paper in half and fold. Make various designs on the fronts and write Christmas greetings inside. Suggestions for designs:

Hand Print of a Small Child: Place the child's hand on the card and trace the outline. Let the child, if old enough, color the hand. This is a goody for grandparents.

Nature Print: Place a leaf on the card, or cut the shape of a butterfly, bird, or animal out of heavy paper or cardboard. Spray the card with spray paint. When dry, remove the leaf or shape.

Christmas Design: Using a cookie cutter, trace a star, reindeer, angel, or lamb on a heavy piece of paper or cardboard. Cut out the shape and place it on the card. Spray paint, or trace and color as a silhouette.

Photo Card: Have some snapshots of the family made for Christmas. Glue these on the front of the cards.

Home-Sketch Card: If someone in your family is artistic, let that person draw a pen sketch of your house. Take this to an offset printer and have your cards made.

Wrapping the Gifts—Let each person go into a separate room, taking plenty of paper (try newspaper, newsprint, or butcher paper—brown or white—as well as traditional paper), scissors, and tape. Let them decorate their own gifts. What a variety!

Decorate the Tree—Using the decorations you made earlier, decorate the tree. Add popcorn strings for an added homemade flavor. Then gather around and read the Christmas story found in Luke 2:1-20. Sing some carols and enjoy the evening.

Hanging of the Greens—This is a great old English custom. You will need a quantity of evergreen twigs and boughs. These are placed over doors, windows, and on the mantel of the fireplace. If you have a fireplace, you will also need some logs. Each member of the family should have a part in "hanging the greens."

As the family is gathering, sing some carols. When everyone has arrived, the family decorates the house with the evergreen boughs and twigs.

Now is the time to light the Yule log. Since few families will have logs as huge as the traditional Yule log, ordinary ones will be fine.

The Christmas tree is now lighted, the Christmas story is read, and more carols are sung.

HOW-TO NIGHT

There are teenagers, as well as children, who may not know how to do some of the simple things adults take for granted. Plan a night to teach some of these to your family. You may be surprised to learn how little some of the members know about these everyday things. Carefully go through each step and explain in full. Although this seems extreme, in many cases it is not. You might divide this project into several family night sessions over the year, but do include it in your planning.

The Telephone—It is of primary importance to teach children to dial correctly, answer the telephone properly, handle a collect call, look up numbers in the telephone book, call long distance (if old enough), handle the phone in case of an emergency (numbers posted), and "let their fingers do the walking" through the yellow pages. With the advent of telecommunications and television telephones, it is possible that there will be an unlimited number of things to be taught.

Appliances—Teach them how to operate the vacuum cleaner; the dishwasher; the blender and mixer; the television (tape machine, movie machine); the washer and dryer; the sewing machine; toaster and other appliances; the calculator; electronic equipment (computer, video games, microwave oven, and whatever else may be in the home).

Financial—Teach them how to write a check; use a credit card; manage money; make a budget; open a savings account. Tell them what the stock market is; how to invest. Give them other financial information—about insurance, loans, interest, etc.

Courtesy—Teach them what manners are and how they work. Explain the courtesies that should be shown to everyone—older adults, parents, teachers, peers. Show them how to set a table; how to use more than one fork; how to carry on a conversation. Good manners will be of value when a child is older.

Sewing—Teach them how to sew on a button and stitch up a ripped seam.

Cooking—Teach them how to cook simple things—eggs, bacon, toast, hamburger; how to cook canned and frozen food; and how to put water back into the water jar when it is empty.

Utilities—Teach them how to cut off the gas or shut off the water or electricity if something goes wrong. Teach them what to do if a fuse blows out or a breaker switch is thrown off; how to change a light bulb in a lamp or ceiling light. Teach them how to unstop a commode. Be sure to emphasize safety when discussing areas involving gas, electricity, and plumbing.

Motorized Vehicles—Teach them how to change a tire, the oil, sparkplugs—the simple maintenance of an automobile; how to operate the lawnmower and change the oil and plug.

MORE SUGGESTIONS FOR
FAMILY NIGHT AT HOME

My Favorite Meal—Let each member of the family request his or her favorite meal on a given night. Since everyone has a turn, everyone must go along with all the other requested menus. If your children are old enough, they might even cook a meal.

Write a Note—Gather paper and pens for everyone. Then decide upon certain people—grandparents, other relatives, close friends—write notes to those people, and mail them. Those who receive the notes will be especially pleased.

Puzzle Night—Purchase a difficult puzzle. The family can spend an evening—or several evenings—around a card table, putting it together.

Game Night—Dig your favorite games out of the closet. The old children's games will bring back memories. If you have no games, visit a store and find the latest challenge.

Video Night—If you own a video set, have a tournament with the video games. Maybe a friend will loan you some cassettes you don't have.

Movie Night—Show a movie on your TV, if you have the equipment. If not, rent a movie from your local library and borrow or rent a projector for the evening. The old movies are the best. Be sure to provide popcorn and soft drinks.

Television Night—Although we do not encourage this, there may occasionally be a program that should be viewed by the entire family. Be very selective in your choices.

Comedy Album Night—Let each member of the family select a favorite comedy record album. As you play them, have a good variety of refreshments.

Write a Book—Sit down as a family, think up a story, and write it down. Who knows—it might be published!

Have a Sing-along—With mother or dad at the piano, sing the old songs and learn some new ones. (See bibliography for songbook suggestions; Vol. 4, *Skits, Plays, and Music,* contains some of the old songs.)

Make a Quilt—Gather up remnants of material and cut them into appropriate sizes and shapes. Obtain the needed materials and purchase, rent, or borrow a quilting frame. Then make a family quilt—you might even make one for each member of the family. These keepsakes will be cherished and may become heirlooms.

Retreat at Home—Select a weekend for a retreat at home. Plan a schedule for study and play and projects. Books for a family to read, study, and enjoy can be found in the bibliography.

Keep in mind that these ideas are but suggestions. Remember that it is vitally important for families to play together, but it is also important for families to pray together. Include God in your family times, through moments of prayer and through the reading of his Holy Word.

2

FUN WITH THE FAMILY

In addition to Family Nights at Home, there are other things a family can enjoy together. These activities will keep you together whether at home or away from the house. A family can create such a positive atmosphere that others will want to join in or imitate. Have fun!

OUTDOOR GAMES

The yard is a perfect place for all types of activities. Even the driveway can be a recreation court for many games. Outside activity is important, and many of the following suggestions can be incorporated in a family night.

Backyard Volleyball—Set up a volleyball net and play as a family, or invite neighbors over to play.

Badminton—Using the same area, play badminton.

Horseshoes—Use the back or side of the yard, away from people and buildings, for this age-old favorite.

Frisbee Golf—Set up a frisbee course around the house, using trash-can lids, old tires, and various other obstacles to make the game challenging.

Kickball—Use basically the same rules as for softball, but players kick the ball instead of hitting it. The pitcher rolls the ball instead of pitching it. A caught fly ball is an out. A runner may be thrown out at a base. It's lots of fun. (For other novelty sports, see Vol. V, *Sports and Outdoor Fun.*)

Broom Hockey—At least eight to ten players are needed. Invite the neighbors! Two teams have an equal number of players and face each other across the playing field. There is a goal at each end of the field (two chairs, cans, etc.). In the middle of the field place two broom sticks and a game ball or volleyball. Number the players on each team; the number one players should be at opposite ends. The referee calls out a number. Both players having that number race to the center of the field, grab the broom sticks and attempt to hit the ball toward each other's goal. When a ball goes through a goal it's a point for the other team. Bring the ball and brooms back to the center of the field. The referee then calls out another number and other players repeat the action. Be sure everyone gets a chance to play.

Four Square—This game is a good one. On a paved driveway, paint or tape a sixteen-foot square and divide it into four equal parts. Number the squares 1, 2, 3, 4. The server stands at square one. One player stands in each of the other squares. If there are more than four players, the extras line up to await a turn when a square is vacated. The object of the game is for the other players to become server. The player who accumulates 21 points wins the game.

The server must serve by bouncing a volleyball or game ball and hitting it underhanded to another player. The player it is hit to cannot return it to the server. Only after the ball has changed hands twice can the server hit the ball. If the ball hits a line, or if a player fails to hit it after it bounces in his or her square or fails to return the ball, the server gets one point and the other player is eliminated from the game. But take heart! The player only goes to the end of the line and will very shortly return. There is no overhand slamming of the ball. Anyone who does this must go to the end of the line.

Frisbee Dodgeball—Same as dodgeball, but use a frisbee. You can also play dodgeball with a ball.

Nerf Tag Football—What could be more fun than Nerf football? Just remember the little ones—they need a chance to score a touchdown.

Golf—By burying small tuna cans up to their rims in your back yard, you can have a miniature golf course. Play for par!

Bowling in the Yard—Using soft-drink bottles and a volleyball, or aluminum cans and a tennis ball, set up your own bowling alley.

CAMPING

Family camping is not new, but it is becoming more popular because many people enjoy going back to a more primitive life-style as well as being outdoors in God's beautiful nature. There are many forms of family camping: You can purchase a large mobile recreation unit with television and all the luxuries and camp on a lake; secure a pop-up camper and travel across the country; pitch a tent at the beach and enjoy the sun; stuff the bare essentials into a backpack and explore beautiful wilderness areas in total seclusion. And there are as many places to go as there are different forms of camping. The advantage of this activity is that the family can work at a common project, growing together while enjoying unique outdoor experiences.

As a family, sit down together and decide on the type of camping you would like. If this will be your first camping adventure, you may want to try it before you purchase any equipment. Many camping outlets will rent equipment so you can discover the kind of camping you enjoy most, or you may be able to borrow equipment from a friend. It is best to camp just overnight, at first, to see how the family adjusts to the great outdoors. Study several camping books, visit campsites, choose your weekend outing wisely.

Shelter

Tent: Every kind, from one-man tents to the large family size can be found at various department or camping stores. Not all tents are waterproof, so ask about that. Although they are not inexpensive, be sure to purchase a quality tent. Some families who are experienced at outdoor wilderness camping use only tent-flies for shelter.

Truck Camper: A pick-up truck with a unit on the truck bed includes basic sleeping facilities. Some are more deluxe, but most are for sleeping and storage only.

Travel Trailer: This vehicle is usually pulled by the family automobile and includes basic sleeping quarters. Some small efficiency campers include refrigerator, sink, and table. This is a very economical and adequate piece of gear.

Recreational Vehicle (RV): This is a mobile home, either pulled by a vehicle or self-contained. It includes all the luxuries—shower, toilet, television, microwave, and so on.

The type of shelter your family decides upon will determine in part the type of camping you will adopt. It would be good to experience all forms of camping before deciding upon one.

Sleeping Gear—In travel trailers or RVs, bedding is usually conventional. For tent camping, you will need sleeping bags and foam pads or air mattresses; if low temperatures are to be encountered, the bags should be northern-goose-down filled, DuPont Fiberfill II, or Polargard filled. Once again, keep quality foremost in mind.

Clothing—Comfortable loose clothing is best. The location of the campsite, the type of camping, and the season dictate the kind of clothing required.

In summer, light-weight clothing may be worn, except in high altitudes. From fall through spring, you will need warm rough clothing that does not show dirt. It is better to peel off clothing than not have adequate protection against the elements.

Sneakers are fine for walking around at the campsite, but for hiking in rough terrain, you should purchase good sturdy hiking boots with lug soles. It is best to wear two pair of wool socks with hiking boots.

NOTE—It is extremely important that you study carefully the camping program you desire to try—the shelter and clothing, the food and cooking gear needed—all the requirements for that type of camping. (A fun idea—cook on a #10 can; see "Family Nights at Home," A Frontier Night.)

Divide Responsibilities—As a team effort, your camping experience can be fun. Give assignments to those children who can carry them out. After the campsite has been chosen, have someone study the brochures from the area and plan places for the family to go and things to see. Another family member can choose travel games. Another can select snacks for the trip. Let the entire family decide upon the menu (or keep it a secret and let a committee decide). Support all family members in their decisions.

Family camping can bring a family closer together when all cooperate in making these days a time to remember. Family devotionals in the great outdoors seem to bring people closer to God and closer together. Take along a good daily devotional book, and find or make up stories to tell. (Several good stories are included in this chapter.)

KITCHEN FUN

Take time to have family fun in the kitchen. Here are some recipes that have been around for years and are still favorites.

BROWN COW
(ROOT BEER FLOAT)

Vanilla ice cream   Root beer, ice cold

Put 1 scoop vanilla ice cream in a tall glass. Slowly fill glass with root beer. Chocolate ice cream may be used to make a **Black Cow**.

PEANUT BUTTER COOKIES

1 cup white sugar	2 cups flour
1 cup brown sugar	1 tsp. soda
1 cup peanut butter	2 eggs, beaten
¾ cup margarine or butter	1 tsp. vanilla

Cream butters and sugars together. Add flour and soda sifted together and mix thoroughly. Add eggs and vanilla and mix well. Place by teaspoonfuls on ungreased cookie sheet and bake 15 minutes in 350° oven.

FANTASY FUDGE

3 cups sugar
¾ cup margarine
⅔ cup (5½ oz. can) evaporated milk
1 tsp. vanilla

1 (12 oz.) pkg. semisweet chocolate bits
1 jar marshmallow creme
1 cup nuts, chopped

Combine sugar, margarine, and milk; bring to a rolling boil, stirring constantly. Boil 5 minutes over medium heat (mixture scorches easily). Remove from heat; add rest of ingredients and stir until chocolate bits are melted. Pour into greased 13 X 9-inch pan. Cool; cut into squares. Makes about 50 small squares.

ICE-CREAM CRUNCH DESSERT

2½ cups crispy cereal, crushed
1 cup flaked coconut
½ cup nuts, chopped

1 cup brown sugar, firmly packed
1 stick butter or margarine, melted
½ gal. ice cream

Mix first five ingredients. Place half of mixture in greased 13 X 9-inch pan. Soften ice cream; beat with mixer. Spread ice cream over crumb mixture and top with remaining crumbs. Freeze. Makes 12 to 16 servings.

PARTY MINTS

1 box (1 lb.) powdered sugar
⅓ cup margarine
⅓ cup white corn syrup

Pinch salt
1 tsp. mint flavoring, or ½ tsp. wintergreen and ½ tsp. peppermint

Place powdered sugar in large bowl; add remaining ingredients. Mix thoroughly. Roll in small balls and place on waxed paper. Press down with a dish or glass dipped in sugar. Layer in box between waxed paper. May be frozen. Makes 125 mints.

CHRISTMAS COOKIES

⅔ cup shortening   1 tsp. vanilla
1¼ cups sugar   3 cups flour
2 eggs   1 tsp. salt
1 T. milk   2 tsp. baking powder

Blend shortening, sugar, eggs, milk, and vanilla. Add combined dry ingredients and mix thoroughly. Roll ⅛ inch thick on lightly floured board and cut with cookie cutter. Bake at 375° on ungreased baking sheets for 8 to 10 minutes or until lightly browned. Remove from pan immediately. Decorate with icing. Makes 6 to 7 dozen cookies.

Icing—Mix confectioner's sugar and water to spreading consistency; add food coloring if desired.

PEANUT BLOSSOMS

1 cup granulated sugar   3½ cups all purpose flour,
1 cup brown sugar, packed   sifted
1 cup butter or margarine   2 tsp. baking soda
1 cup creamy peanut   1 tsp. salt
  butter   2 (10 oz.) pkgs. chocolate
2 eggs   kisses
¼ cup milk
2 tsp. vanilla

Cream sugars and butters. Beat in eggs, milk, and vanilla. Sift together flour, soda, and salt; stir into egg mixture. Shape into balls; roll in additional granulated sugar. Place on ungreased baking sheet; bake in 375° oven for 10 to 12 minutes. Immediately press a chocolate candy into each cookie. Makes 7 dozen.

OATMEAL COOKIES

¾ cup shortening

1 cup brown sugar, firmly
  packed

½ cup granulated sugar

1 egg

¼ cup water

1 tsp. vanilla

3 cups oatmeal, uncooked

1 cup all-purpose flour

1 tsp. salt

½ tsp. soda

Preheat oven to 350°. Beat together shortening, sugars, egg, water, and vanilla until creamy. Add combined remaining ingredients; mix well. Drop by rounded teaspoonfuls onto greased cookie sheet. Bake at 350° for 10 to 12 minutes. Makes about 5 dozen.

STRAWBERRY SLUSH

½ cup strawberries,
  frozen or fresh

¼ cup strawberry juice
  or water

½ cup nonfat dry milk

ice cubes (until blender is
  full)

sugar substitute

Blend first three ingredients in blender. Add ice cubes one at a time, blending after each addition. Add sugar substitute to taste.

CANDY KISSES

3 egg whites

⅛ tsp. salt

3½ T. gelatin (½ box)

¾ cup sugar

1 T. vinegar

1 cup chocolate bits

Beat egg whites with salt until foamy. Gradually add gelatin and sugar. Beat to stiff peaks, making sure sugar is well dissolved or kisses will be sticky. Mix in vinegar. Fold in chocolate bits. Drop by teaspoonfuls onto ungreased cookie sheet lined with brown paper. Bake 25 minutes at 250°. Turn off the oven but leave the kisses right where they are for another 20 minutes. Makes about 7 dozen.

BROWNIES

1 egg	1 cup flour, sifted
1 cup chocolate syrup	½ cup sugar
½ cup butter	½ tsp. salt
or margarine	½ cup nuts, chopped

Mix egg, chocolate syrup, and butter thoroughly. Sift together flour, sugar, and salt. Stir the dry mixture into the wet and add nuts. Pour batter into 8- or 9-inch square pan. Bake 30 minutes at 350°. Cool and cut into squares.

LEMON ICE-BOX PIE

Vanilla wafers	Juice of 3 lemons
1 can sweetened	Whipped cream or whipped
condensed milk	topping

Crumble vanilla wafers in bottom of pie pan. Line sides with whole wafers. Mix condensed milk and lemon juice together until juice has blended with milk. Pour mixture in pie pan, smooth, and top with whipped cream or topping. Place in refrigerator.

POPCORN CAKE

3 quarts unsalted popcorn,	1 (10 oz.) pkg.
popped	marshmallows
1 stick butter	1 tsp. vanilla
or margarine	1 can mixed nuts
	1 pkg. spice gumdrops

Melt butter or margarine and marshmallows together. Add vanilla. Stir popcorn into mixture. Add nuts and gumdrops. Pack mixture firmly into buttered tube pan. Make sure it is packed tightly. Let set overnight (or at least 4 hours).

INDOOR GAMES

Modeling—Give everyone a stick of chewing gum, a white card, and two toothpicks. After the gum has been chewed to the proper consistency, each person proceeds to mold an animal, a bust, or whatever the imagination dictates. The result is mounted on the card, the modeler's name is signed to it, and all the cards are put on display.

Fisherman—Players gather around a table or sit on the ground. One player is the Fisherman, who has a short stick to which is attached a piece of twine with a loop at its end. The Fisherman drops the line in such a way that the loop lies on the table, near center. When the Fisherman says "Whose fish?" all players put the tips of their forefingers on the table inside the circle formed by the twine. Suddenly the Fisherman calls "My fish!" and pulls in the line. Players try to withdraw their fingers before they are caught in the loop. The Fisherman must pull in the line very quickly in order to catch anything. Each player is Fisherman in turn.

Fire—The person in the center of a ring of players points a finger at one of the players, shouts either "Earth!" or "Air!" or "Water!" or "Fire!" and counts to ten.

The person pointed to must answer appropriately before IT can count to ten. If "Earth" was called, some quadruped (horse, cow, dog, mule, etc.) must be named. If "Water," it must be some denizen of the deep (whale, shark, perch, turtle, etc.). If "Air," some bird or flying insect. If "Fire" was called, the player must remain silent.

Variation: A ball or knotted handkerchief may be thrown to the player who is to respond.

Drawing Animals—Each player is given a slip of paper and a pencil. At the top of the paper, write the name of an animal. Turn this part under so that the name cannot be seen by the others. Then draw a picture of that animal. When finished each person exhibits the work of art. After others have guessed at what it is, turn back the flap so they can see what you have tried to draw.

Variation: Pass the slips to the right. Each player draws whatever is indicated on the slip.

Bubble Blowing—You can have a lot of bubble fun. Use clay pipes or regular bubble pipes.

Stunts:

1. See who can blow:
    the bubble that goes highest;
    the bubble that lasts longest;
    the largest bubble;
    the most bubbles from one dip.

2. Two people can blow one bubble by holding their pipes close together and allowing their bubbles to merge into one bubble. Try this with three or four blowers.

3. Fan bubbles through a hoop or wicket.

Play Bubble Tennis: Players fan their bubbles over a table-tennis net. A bubble that lands on the table on the other side of the net scores a point. Opposing players do not try to prevent bubbles from landing.

Play Bubble Croquet: Fan bubbles through seven wickets on a table.

Wickets can be made of pieces of wire stuck in spools. A player blows a bubble and fans it through the first wicket. If successful, player blows another bubble and fans it through the second wicket. Same player continues until unsuccessful. Then another player takes a turn. The first player to get a bubble through each wicket wins.

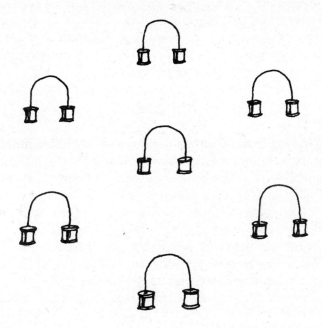

Jackstraws—This old game requires steadiness of nerves. Jackstraws may be made of matches, or tiny sticks or twigs anywhere from two to six inches long. It would be better for all sticks to be of uniform length. A match with a pin in the end, bent into a hook, will do for a lifter. A player holds a handful of jackstraws in a closed fist and drops them to the table from a distance of ten inches. Then the first player takes the lifter and tries to lift one of the "straws" without disturbing any of the others. When that player fails, another player takes a turn. The one with the most sticks wins.

Piling High—Give each child a box of flat toothpicks and one soft-drink bottle. See how many toothpicks can be stacked on top of the bottle.

Variation: Give children twenty-five toothpicks apiece and one bottle. They take turns, each placing one toothpick on the bottle at a turn. If a player knocks off any toothpicks, they are added to that player's pile. The player whose toothpicks are used up first wins.

BRAIN TEASERS

The Dog and the Rabbit—A dog chasing a rabbit makes two 10-foot jumps every second, while the rabbit makes three. The dog would have caught the rabbit in just 10 minutes had nothing prevented.

But 10 seconds before the dog would have caught up, a shot from a hunter's gun killed the bunny. At the time of the shot the rabbit was only 20 feet ahead of the dog.

What was the distance between the dog and the rabbit at the start of the chase?

Answer: 1,200 feet. The dog was gaining 2 feet per second—120 feet a minute: 1,200 feet in 10 minutes.

The Fish Tale—A big city fish merchant once offered a 20 percent reduction on a fish that weighed "10 pounds and half its weight," if the buyer could tell him how much the fish actually weighed. What *did* it weigh?

Answer: 20 pounds.

The Pawnshop Brain Teaser—Mr. A. owed Mr. B. $10, but he had only $7. Mr. A. decided to do some juggling. So he took a $5 bill to the pawnshop and obtained a $4 loan. Next, he took the pawn ticket to Mr. C. who, knowing the ticket represented $5 in currency, purchased it for $4. Now Mr. A. had the necessary $10 to pay his debt. Who lost in the transaction?

Answer: Mr. C. He overlooked the fact that he would have to pay $4 to the pawn broker to redeem the $5 bill. Thus he paid $8 for the $5 bill, losing $3.

The Spook Train—Two men were on the Spook Train bound for Eternity Station. One of them had been a very wicked man. The other had been a very good man. When it was almost time for the conductor to take up their tickets, the wicked man became increasingly nervous. Finally he said to the good man, "I have no ticket. Can you help me?"

The good man answered, "Yes, I think I can." He tore off part of his ticket on one side and then on the other, after folding it.

"But this isn't enough ticket for me," said the evil man. "Why not give me more?" So the good man tore off two more pieces and gave them to him.

The conductor came by, opened the folded tickets, and this is what he saw: The good man's ticket was in the form of a cross. The bad man's ticket spelled H-E-L-L.

The Manner of Folding and Tearing: Take a piece of paper about a third as wide as it is long. Fold over one-third. Now fold over the ends to a point at the middle of the double thickness part of the paper. Then fold back the top end (single thickness). Holding the pointed piece, tear off a strip about one-fifth of the width. Repeat on other side. Then repeat the action and unfold.

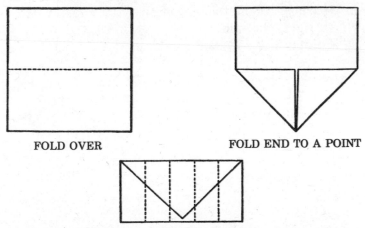

FOLD OVER   FOLD END TO A POINT

FOLD OVER SINGLE END AND TEAR ON DOTTED LINES

The Monkey Teaser—Four monkeys can eat 4 sacks of peanuts in 3 minutes. How many monkeys will it take to eat 100 sacks of peanuts in 60 minutes?

Answer: 5. If 4 monkeys can eat 4 sacks of peanuts in 3 minutes, 1 monkey can eat 1 sack of peanuts in 3 minutes. In 60 minutes, 1 monkey could eat 20 sacks of peanuts. Thus it would take 5 monkeys to eat 100 sacks of peanuts in 60 minutes. It is, of course, taken for granted that a monkey has the capacity to consume 20 sacks of peanuts.

The King's Arithmetic Problem—Once there lived a clever king. One day there came to his court a professor who delighted the king with his knowledge. He entertained the ruler with many things that were new and interesting.

The king wanted to know the age of the professor, but he hesitated to ask. So he propounded a mathematical problem.

"Professor," said the king, "I have an interesting problem for you. It is a test in mental arithmetic. Think of the number of the month of your birth, but don't tell me." Now the professor was 60 years old, and his birthday came in December. So he thought of 12.

"All right," he said.

"Multiply it by 2," said the king.

"I have."

"Add 5."

"I have."

"Now multiply by 50."

"Yes."

"Add your age."

"Yes."

"Subtract 365."

"Yes."

"Add 115."

"Yes."

"And now," said the king, "tell me the result."

"Twelve hundred and sixty," replied the professor.

"Thank you," said the king. "You were born in December sixty years ago."

"But how do you know that?" cried the professor.

"From your answer," replied the king. "You said it was 1,260. The month of birth was 12 and the last two figures gave your age."

"Well," laughed the professor, "that is a polite way to find out one's age."

Fun with Dominoes—Play the regular game, allowing no playing on spinners except when the player can score a 5 or multiple of 5.

Variation: **Forty-two**—Four players. Each player draws seven dominoes. Players bid in turn, 30, 32, or the perfect score 42. The player who gets the bid names trump—that is, the dominant number. Doubles take any trick of their kind. Doubles can also be trump, in which case they no longer belong to the rest of their numbers. Points are made by taking the 5 + 5, the 6 + 4, the 5 + 0, the 4 + 1, and the 3 + 2. That totals 35. One point is allowed for each trick. Since there are seven possible tricks, that makes a total of 7 points; 42 thus is the perfect score. A player who is confident of taking all the tricks may bid 84 (2 × 42). Or a player may bid "Nullo," in which case the player cannot take any tricks. Hands are played like bridge or rook. Except for trump, highest end of domino determines suit.

The Animals and the Circus—The animals went to the circus. They had to have some money to get in.

The duck got in. Why? It had a bill.

The frog got in. It had a greenback.

The deer got in. It had a buck (*or* the doe).

The hog got in. It had four quarters.

The skunk did not get in, although it had a (s)cent. (But it was a bad one.)

The Ranch Story—A father bought a ranch and presented it to his two sons. They planned to raise cattle for the market. So they called the ranch Focus. Why was that an appropriate name?

Answer: That's where the sun's rays meet (sons raise meat).

How's Your Dog? A lawyer was in the habit of walking to his office. One morning as he passed the home of a certain woman, her vicious bulldog attacked him. The lawyer kicked the dog to protect himself. His foot landed squarely on the dog's head and laid it out cold.

The next day he stopped at the same house and rang the doorbell. When the woman came to the door he said, "Lady, house your dog." She answered, "I did."

Nine out of ten people will think the question is, "Lady, how's your dog?"

The Three Condemned Men—A penitentiary warden, seeking pardons for three men, was told by the governor that only one could be pardoned, the warden to decide which one. Wishing to give all three an equal chance, the warden called them in and explained the situation. "I shall seat you around a table and bindfold all three of you," he said. "Then I shall place on each forehead either a black or a red mark. When I remove the blindfolds you are to start rapping on the table if you see black on either or both the foreheads of the other two men. The first man who can name his own color and give his reasons satisfactorily will be the one who is pardoned."

He blindfolded the men and placed black marks on all their foreheads. When the blindfolds were removed, all three men naturally began rapping.

After an interval of two or three minutes, one man stopped. "Warden, my color is black," he said. He explained his reason for knowing his color, and he was freed. How did he know his color was black?

Answer: He reasoned in this way: If my color were red, we would still all three be knocking as the other men would be knocking for each other. But they could see I was black, and one or the other would realize immediately that the third man was knocking for him. If I were red, one of the other two men would have announced immediately that he was black. Since neither did, they must be mystified, and I am obviously black.

Dollar, Dollar, Who's Got the Dollar?—Three men spent several nights in a hotel. When they were ready to check out, they found that their bill was $30, $10 each. They sent the money down to the desk by a bellboy. When he paid the cashier, he was told that since the hotel was run on the cooperative plan, the men had $5 coming back to them. The bellboy kept $2 and handed each of the men $1. That meant each man paid $9. Three times nine is twenty-seven. Add this to the $2 retained by the bellboy and you have $29. Where did the other dollar go?

Answer: The men paid $25 to the hotel and $2 to the bellboy. That totals $27. The $3 that was refunded to them makes $30.

August—August was a hound pup who was always jumping at conclusions. One day he jumped at the conclusion of a stubborn mule. And the next day was the first of September. How do we know the day?

Answer: Because that was the last of August.

Masticate!—The small son of a college professor was taken to the railroad station. He was greatly thrilled by what he saw, and when a big engine came roaring into the station, he jumped up and down in his excitement and yelled, "Masticate! Masticate!" What did he mean?

Answer: Chew! Chew! (choo-choo).

Too Wise—

YY U R, YY U B;
I C U R YY 4 me.
(Too wise you are, too wise you be;
I see you are too wise for me.)

Pronounce T-O—Pronounce *T-O*. Now *T-O-O*. Now *T-W-O*. Now the second day of the week. Almost invariably the response will be "Tuesday." But the second day of the week is Monday.

A Series of Macs—Pronounce *M-A-C-D-O-U-G-A-L*. Now pronounce *M-A-C-D-O-N-A-L-D*. Now pronounce *M-A-C-H-I-N-E-R-Y*. Most people will pronounce the *C* as *K*.

Four Nines—Write four nines so that they make an even hundred.
Answer: 99 9/9.

Match Tricks—

1. Make three squares, using ten matches. Now subtract two matches and leave two squares.
Answer: Take away the matches numbered 1 and 2.

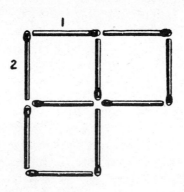

2. Place sixteen matches in four squares. Move three and subtract four, and spell the word that indicates what matches are made of.

Answer: LOVE.

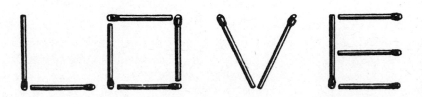

3. Make four triangles out of six matches.

Answer: One is laid flat on the table. The other three are held pyramid-like about this triangle, making four triangles.

4. Take twelve matches and form six triangles.

Answer: Form a hexagon with six of the matches. Then use the other six from the center of the hexagon to form the sides of the triangles.

5. Arrange twelve matches in four squares. Rearrange the matches to form three squares, using all matches, but moving only three of them.

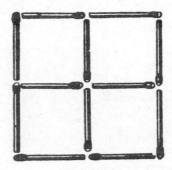

Answer: Remove the two matches from the upper left-hand corner and the lower match in the lower right-hand corner. Use these three matches to form a new square at the lower right.

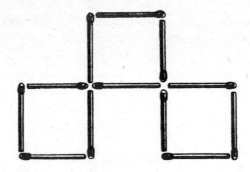

Match Squares—Arrange twenty-four matches in nine squares, making one big square. Then remove six matches and leave three complete squares.

Answer: Take any six consecutive matches marked with an X. That will leave the center square, one corner square, and the large square.

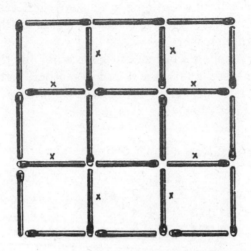

Variations:

(a) To remove four matches and leave seven squares, take any four outside corner matches.

(b) To remove four matches and leave six squares, remove two matches from the center square and two adjacent matches from a corner square.

(c) To remove four matches and leave five squares, remove all four center square matches.

What Relation to You Is—

Your sister-in-law's father-in-law's granddaughter? (niece)

Your uncle's father's father's wife? (great-grandmother)

Your mother's aunt's brother's wife? (great-aunt)
The grandson of the only son of your mother's mother-in-law? (son or nephew)
Your brother's mother's stepson's father? (stepfather)
Your sister's son's brother's father? (brother-in-law)
Your aunt's father's only grandson? (yourself)
Your mother's mother's son's son? (first cousin)
Your sister-in-law's husband's grandfather's wife? (grandmother)
Your nephew's father's father's wife? (mother)
Your sister's father's stepson's mother? (stepmother)
Brothers and sisters have I none—but this man's father is my father's son. (son)

That's One on You—

$$1 \times 9 + 2 = \qquad 11$$
$$12 \times 9 + 3 = \qquad 111$$
$$123 \times 9 + 4 = \qquad 1111$$
$$1{,}234 \times 9 + 5 = \qquad 11111$$

Continue to figure in this same manner on up to 12,345,678. You will find that this number, times 9, plus 9, equals 111,111,111.

What's 8-ing You?—

$$9 \times 0 + 8 = \qquad 8$$
$$9 \times 9 + 7 = \qquad 88$$
$$9 \times 98 + 6 = \qquad 888$$
$$9 \times 987 + 5 = \qquad 8888$$

Following this same system, you finally come to 9 times 98,765,432 plus 0, which equals 888,888,888. And then you will find that 9 times 987,654,321, minus 1, equals 8,888,888,888.

The Winning Nine—

$$9 \times 9 = 81$$
$$99 \times 99 = 9,801$$
$$999 \times 999 = 998,001$$
$$9,999 \times 9,999 = 99,980,001$$
$$99,999 \times 99,999 = 9,999,800,001$$

Sequences—

$$1 \times 8 + 1 = 9$$
$$12 \times 8 + 2 = 98$$
$$123 \times 8 + 3 = 987$$

And thus it will go until 123,456,789 times 8, plus 9, equals 987,654,321.

Six Numbers Six Times—Note that the same numbers are used each time. Note also their sequence. Take the number 142,857. Multiply by 2 and you have 285,714. Multiply by 3 and you get 428,571. Multiply by 4 and the result is 571,428. Five times 142,857 gives you 714,285. Six times the number makes 857,142. Note than when you multiply by 6 the two sets of numbers are transposed. Multiply by 7 and note the result.

Take a Number—

Number selected...................................	23
Double it..	46
Add 1...	47
Multiply by 5..	235
Add 5...	240
Multiply by 10..	2,400
Subtract 100..	2,300

Strike off the last two digits. The number is 23.

Your Pocket Change—Think of a number (your age, perhaps). Double it. Add five. Multiply by 50. Add the change (less than a dollar) in your pocket. Subtract the number of days in a year. Add 115. Example:

2 × your age..	38
Add 5..	43
Multiply by 50.......................................	2,150
Add the 21 cents in your pocket..........	2,171
Subtract 365..	1,806
Add 115...	1,921

Your age is 19 and the amount of change in your pocket is 21 cents.

Number, Please!—Select a number or use your age.

Number selected.....................................	27
Multiply by 3..	81
Add 1..	82
Multiply by 3..	246
Add original number..............................	273
Strike off last digit................................	27

Age and Month of Birth—Think of the number of the month of your birth.

Month of birth (April)............................	4
Double it...	8
Add 5..	13
Multiply by 50.......................................	650
Add your age (21)...................................	671
Subtract 365..	306
Add 115...	421

The first one or two digits indicate the month and the last two indicate the age.

I've Got Your Number—Write the number 1,089 on a slip of paper and hand it to someone to hold. Then ask someone to write down any number of three different digits. Reverse this number and subtract the smaller from the larger. If only two digits result, add a cipher to make three. Then reverse this result and add.

The number given	456
Reversed	654
Smaller subtracted from larger	198
Reverse this result	891
Add last two figures	1,089

Secret Number—Select a number.

Number selected	13
Double it	26
Multiply by 5	130
Take off last digit	13

What's Your Number?—Take a number. Double it. Add 9. Subtract 3. Divide by 2. Subtract the secret number. The answer is 3.

Or take a number. Double it. Add 12. Subtract 4. Divide by 2. Subtract the secret number. The answer is 4.

The number in each case will always be one half of the difference between the number added and the number subtracted. If the number added is smaller than the number subtracted in step four, the resulting number will be a minus.

How Many Apples Did Adam and Eve Eat?—A group was discussing this question. The first person said it couldn't have been more than 1. A second person asserted that Eve 8 (ate), and Adam 2 (too)—a total of 10. The third person said there was something wrong about that because Eve 8 and Adam 8 also, making 16. "But," said another, "if Eve 8 and Adam 8-2, that would be a total of 90." Still another chimed in: "According to antedeluvian history, Eve 8-1 and Adam 8-2. That would total 163." "But," contended another, "don't you see that if Eve 8-1 and Adam 8-1-2, that would be a total of 893." "According to my figuring I calculate that if Eve 8-1-4 Adam and Adam 8-1-2-4 Eve, that would total 8,938." "Yes," said the remaining member of the group, "but the best mathematicians agree that if Eve 8-1-4 Adam and if Adam 8-1-2-2 oblige Eve, the total would be 8,936." "Meeting adjourned," announced the chairman.

A Digit Fit—The answers to the following questions must contain digits. Example: What made Willie sick? While eating apples he 8-1-2 green.

1. Why did you come here tonight?
   Answer: Just 4 fun, *or* We came 2-8-10 the party.
2. How do we know that Noah was preceded from the ark by at least three people?
   Answer: Because the Bible says that Noah came 4th (forth).
3. Why is there so little cake left?
   Answer: You 8-2 much, *or* You 8-2 be4 I 8-1.
4. How old are you?
   Answer: That's 0 (nothing) 2 you.
5. What digit rhymes with frauds?
   Answer: 6, because it rhymes with tricks.
6. Who is the victor?
   Answer: The 1 who 1.
7. When do we eat?
   Answer: That remains 2 be seen.

Hands—Answers must contain the word *hand.*

1. A hand for the acrobat.
2. A hand for the monkey.
3. A hand that assures you'll never have need of a donkey.
4. A hand for the criminal.
5. A hand that's for play.
6. A hand for measuring.

7. For the wedding day.
8. A hand for the creative.
9. One for those who toil.
10. A hand for letters.
11. A hand you often soil.
12. A hand that's good-looking.
13. A hand for a bike.
14. A hand that is useful on hammer or spade.
15. A hand that's improvident.
16. A hand that supports.
17. A hand that advertises.
18. One useful in jobs and sports.

Answers: (1) handspring (2) hand-organ (3) handcart (4) handcuff (5) handball (6) handbreath (7) handmaiden (8) handicraft (9) handwork (10) handwriting (11) handkerchief (12) handsome (13) handlebar (14) handle (15) hand-to-mouth (16) handrail (17) handbill (18) handy

Heads—The answers contain the word *head*.

1. A head that glows.
2. One that brings woes.
3. A head the football player knows.
4. A head that pains.
5. A head that gains.
6. A head that marks the dead's remains.
7. A head that's food.
8. A head that's rude.
9. A head that usually is nude.
10. A head for the printer.
11. A head that is center.
12. A head that seats the crowd for dinner.
13. A head that flows.
14. A head that goes.
15. A head that every woman shows.

Answers: (1) headlight (2) headstrong (3) headgear (4) headache (5) headway (6) headstone (7) headcheese (8) heady (9) head hunter (*or* bald head) (10) headline (11) headquarters (12) head waiter (13) headwater (14) head race (15) headdress

Feet—The answers are words containing the word *foot*.

1. A foot to buy a barefoot guy.
2. A foot that tells someone's close by.
3. A foot on a page.
4. A foot on a stage.
5. A foot that when friendly is good for any age.
6. A foot that steals.
7. A foot that feels.
8. A foot that woe to cattle wields.
9. A foot that's tired.
10. A foot that's hired.
11. A foot by grandma oft desired.
12. A foot that is free.
13. And one we all agree is a very good game we like to see.

Answers: (1) footwear (2) footfall (3) footnote (4) footlight (5) footing (6) footpad (7) footsore (8) foot-and-mouth disease (9) footworn (10) footman (11) footstool (12) foot-loose (13) football

STORYTELLING

Storytelling is an art as old as the human race. Everyone in all the world, old and young alike, responds to a good story.

Stories are important to children: They satisfy the craving of the imagination; they serve to introduce children to the world in which they live; they are children's first introduction to literature. Thus good stories are an essential part of a child's development.

The child's part in storytelling involves listening, commenting, asking questions, joining in the telling, retelling, telling other stories, inventing stories, and playing out the stories.

Pointers—The storyteller should have a real enthusiasm for the stories. A story should be told with appreciation for its dramatic qualities and should build to its proper climax.

A good story is its own excuse for being told. The storyteller should not point out the moral. Remember Henry Van Dyke's prayer: "Grant, Lord, that I may never tag a moral to a tale, or tell a story without a meaning."

HOW THE SUN, MOON, AND STARS CAME INTO THE SKY

Long long ago, the Indians had no fire and no light. They suffered much during the cold of winter, and they had to eat their food raw. They also lived in darkness because there was no light.

There were no sun, moon, or stars in the sky. A great chief kept them all locked up in a box. He took great pride that he alone had light.

This great chief had a beautiful daughter of whom he also was proud. She was much beloved by all the Indians of the tribe.

The raven was a great friend of the Indians and wondered how it might make life more comfortable for them. In those days some Indians believed that the raven had magic powers.

One day, the raven saw the daughter of the chief come down to the brook for a drink. It had an idea. It would change itself into a pine needle on a tree that spread its branches out over the brook. So the next time the maiden came to drink, it dropped into the brook and was swallowed by her.

As time went on the raven was born to her as a son. The old chief was delighted, and as the boy grew, his grandfather became devoted to him. Anything he wanted he could have.

One day the boy asked the old chief for the box containing the stars. Reluctantly the old chief gave it to him. The child played for awhile by rolling the box around. Then he released the stars and flung them into the sky.

The Indians were delighted. Now there was some light, though not enough.

After a few days the child asked for the box containing the moon. The chief demurred, but by insistence the boy got what he wanted. Again, after playing for awhile with the box, the boy released the moon and flung it into the sky.

The tribesmen were overjoyed. But still there was not light enough. And anyway, the moon disappeared for long periods.

So finally the child asked for the box with the sun. "No," said the old chief, "I cannot give you that." But the boy wept and pleaded. The old chief could not withstand his tears and finally gave it to him. And as soon as he had a chance, the child released the sun and cast it into the sky.

The joy of the Indians knew no bounds. Here was light enough, and warmth as well. So they ordered a feast in honor of the sun and all the Indians celebrated with great jubilation.

And the old chief was happy. He had not known that the sun, moon, and stars could bring so much comfort and happiness to his people. And for the first time, he himself enjoyed them.

HOW OLD MAN CREATED THE RACES
(CREE INDIAN)

Once upon a time Old Man lived all alone, except for the animals. But their companionship was not satisfying. Old Man was lonesome and longed for company. So he said, "I'll make a man."

He made a great big earth oven and built a fire in it. Then he took some clay and molded it into the form of a man. He put this into the oven. But when he took it out, it was not done. It had not stayed in long enough. This clay man became father of all of the white races.

Again the Great One made a clay man and put it into the oven. This time when he took it out it was burned black. It had stayed in too long. This clay man became father of the black races.

With great care he formed a third man of clay and put it into the oven. This time he watched it carefully and took it out when it had baked to a perfect brown. It was just right.

This third clay man became the father of the Red Man, the Indian.

THE FABLE OF THE SCORPION
(AFRICAN)

Since the scorpion hides its head, it seems to have no face. Do you know why it has no face?

In the beginning of time God created all the animals. Last of all, he gave each of them a head and face.

One day it was appointed that all the animals should report to a certain spot, where the distribution of heads was to be made. All the animals started out on the journey.

But the scorpion was slower than the others, so as it labored along the road the other animals passed it. When it was still not more than half way, it met the screech owl coming back. And what a sight it was! The owl's face looked as if it had been shoved in and not pulled out again.

The scorpion stopped the owl and looked at it in amazement.

"Hello," greeted the screech owl. "You had better hurry or you'll get there too late to get a face."

"What is that you have on your shoulders?" asked the scorpion, looking puzzled.

"Oh, that's my head and face. Isn't it handsome?" said the screech owl.

"Goodness gracious!" exclaimed the scorpion. "Is that what they're giving out?"

"Why, yes!" responded the screech owl. "Everyone gets one."

"Well, excuse me," said the scorpion. "I don't believe I want one, so I'm not going."

THE CAMEL AND THE JACKAL
(HINDU)

In the long ago when animals could talk, there were a camel and a jackal who were good friends.

Now the camel loved sugar cane and the jackal dearly loved crabs. Just across the river was a fine cane field, and nearby there were lots of crabs and other delicacies to tickle the palate of the jackal.

"I cannot swim," said the jackal. "How about taking me across the river on your back? There's plenty of juicy sugar cane over there." So the camel let the jackal hop on his back and away they went.

The jackal jumped off as soon as they were across and fell to on the crabs. He was a fast eater and had stuffed himself with crabs and fish before the camel could get a good start on the sugar cane. Then he began to jump and run about yelping, making a terrible racket.

Some men in the village nearby heard the noise. They sounded the alarm, and many men came running. They couldn't catch the jackal, but they did catch the camel, and they beat him unmercifully.

When the men left, the jackal ran up to the camel and said, "Let us go home."

"I guess we had better," groaned the camel. "Climb up on my back and let us start."

When they came to the place were the water was deep,

the camel said, "Why did you make such a racket before I had hardly gotten a mouthful of sugar cane?"

"Oh," answered the jackal, "that's just an old habit of mine. I always sing after I have been well fed."

The water was getting deeper and deeper and in another step the camel would be compelled to swim.

"You know," said the camel, "I feel like taking a roll."

"Oh, don't do that," exclaimed the jackal. "You know I can't swim."

"Well, I guess I'll roll," again said the camel.

"Please don't!" begged the jackal. "Why in the world would you want to roll?"

"Well, you see," answered the camel, "it is just an old habit of mine. I always like to roll after dinner."

And roll he did, and you can guess what happened to the jackal. Some say he drowned. Others say the camel finally pulled him out and left him exhausted on the shore, coughing up water and trying hard to get his breath.

WHY DOGS AND CATS ARE ENEMIES
(CHINESE)

Once upon a time a Chinese dog and a Chinese cat lived with an old Chinese man and woman. The old man and woman had a magic wishing ring which meant everything to them. But the ring had been stolen by robbers and they were very sad.

It seems the robbers had gone across the river and were in hiding on the other side. So the cat said to the dog, "I cannot swim, but if you will carry me across the river on your back, maybe we can find the robbers and get the ring back."

At that time the dog and cat were good friends. Therefore the dog answered, "Why certainly. By all means, we must get the ring back for our heartbroken masters." So he took the cat on his back and swam across.

They soon found the robbers and discovered that the ring was hidden in a wooden chest. So the cat caught a mouse, who gnawed a hole in the chest so the cat could bring out the ring. Then the dog took the cat on his back and swam back across the river.

They started for home, but the cat then left the dog and climbed over the roofs of houses. The dog had to go around through the streets and alleys, because dogs cannot climb, you know.

Therefore the cat reached home first and returned the ring to its owners. He never told the part the dog had played in the recovery of the ring. The old Chinese man and woman were delighted. They petted and patted the cat and gave him cream to drink.

When the dog got home, they scolded him for being away so long and for being wet and muddy. The old woman took the broom to him.

So the dog chased the cat up a tree. And ever since, dogs and cats have been enemies.

THE BELLMAKER
(CHINESE)

Long ago a certain province in China was famous for its bells. Now the average Chinese bell is not like ours—it is struck with a gong rather than by a swinging clapper. The fame of the bells of this province was due to the skill of one particular bellmaker. He even achieved official distinction because of the richness of tone sounded by the metal in the gongs he was able to produce from his molds.

One day the ruler of the province summoned the bell-maker to his court. "Make me," he said, "a bell that has in its tones the mellowness of gold, the music of silver, and the depth and resonance of brass. Furthermore, the sound must be heard for at least three miles."

The bellmaker went home sad at heart, for he feared he could never fulfill this command. Nevertheless he set his men to work and finally the day of the test came. The ruler of the province was there with his retinue. The molten metal poured through the runway into the mold, and all awaited the final proof when the gong should sound forth its magic tones. None in the great crowd watched more anxiously than Kong Gay, the bellmaker's lovely young daughter. But it was as the bellmaker had feared. His efforts were in vain, for this was no magic bell with the mellowness of gold and the music of silver and the resonance of brass.

The ruler was angry and declared that he had lost face before the whole world for he had boasted of the skill of one who had proved himself unworthy. The bellmaker pleaded for another chance and finally his plea was granted.

Alas, the second trial was no better than the first. This time the ruler was so infuriated that he threatened to execute such an inferior artisan. Finally, however, he was persuaded to grant one more trial. But if that should fail, the bellmaker's life would be forfeit.

Poor little Kong Gay realized the hopelessness of her father's case. Twice he had tried, and twice he had failed. Something must be done or he would lose his life. So under cover of night she slipped away to consult a soothsayer. Perhaps he could help her find some way to save her father.

When the fortuneteller heard her story, he was silent for awhile. Then he said, "The only thing that will make a bell with such a miraculous tone is human flesh molded in the metal, and this would mean the sacrifice of a life." Kong Gay returned home without telling anyone what she had heard.

The morning of the great day arrived when the last run of molten metal was to be poured from the immense cauldron. Above the runway a platform had been constructed, and on it stood the bellmaker, his daughter Kong Gay, her amah, and other attendants.

As the red-hot molten liquid came streaming beneath them, Kong Gay suddenly cried out, "For you, my father," and leaped downward into the fiery stream. As she sprang, the amah screamed and tried to hold her, but all she caught in her hand was a tiny silken shoe.

The father, in his horror, tried to leap after his daughter, and only the combined efforts of his attendants restrained him from plunging off the platform.

The metal cooled and a silent audience awaited the sound of the great gong. Suddenly it rang forth, sounding out across the miles a magic tone which had all the mellowness of gold, all the musical peals of silver, and all the strength and resonance of brass. But that was not all! There was also the distinct sound of a plaintive voice, as if calling, "Kong-g-g Gay-y-y! Hai Yai!"

"Ah!" the listeners cried. "It is Kong Gay. She is calling for her slipper. It is Kong Gay, calling for her little silken shoe."

And today if you go to that province and to that city, you will hear the great bell. The children in the streets stop their play as it sounds forth at noon. "Listen," they will tell you. "Listen to Kong Gay. She is calling for her little silken shoe."

THE DUCK'S DISTRESS

Clap when the word Doctor *or* Drake *is mentioned. If mentioned together, clap twice. Be careful not to clap at any other time.*

Once upon a time a duck caught a cold, or what he thought was a cold. "I must go to a doctor" (clap once), said he. "What doctor (clap once) shall it be?"

"Try Doctor Drake" (clap twice), advised a friend. So he went to Doctor Drake (clap twice).

The doctor (clap once) looked the duck over carefully, made him say "ah" while he looked down his throat, thumped his chest, looked stern, and then said, "Hmm! You've got the epizoodic."

"The what?" said the duck.

"The epizoodic, no more nor less," answered Doctor Drake (clap twice).

This made the duck angry. "What a doctor!" (clap once) he stormed. "I'll go to a quack doctor (clap once) and he will fix me up as good as new."

"Suit yourself," said Doctor Drake (clap twice).

So the duck went to see a quack doctor (clap once). "Hmm! Looks like the epizoodic," said the quack doctor (clap once).

"The what?" said the duck.

"The epizoodic, no more and no less," replied the quack doctor (clap once).

"Aw, go chase yourself," said the duck. "I'll go to another doctor" (clap once).

So he went to a famous eye, ear, nose, and throat specialist. This doctor (clap once) looked serious, made the duck open his mouth, peered down into it, shook his head and said, "Hmm! It looks like you have the epizoodic."

"The what?" said the duck.

"The epizoodic, no more and no less," answered the doctor (clap once).

"What shall I do?" asked the duck.

"There's only one doctor (clap once) who can cure that," answered the doctor (clap once).

"And who is that?" asked the duck.

"Doctor Drake (clap twice). Yes, Doctor Drake (clap twice) is the great epizoodic specialist. You'd better go to Doctor Drake" (clap twice).

So the duck hurried back to Doctor Drake (clap twice) and Doctor Drake (clap twice) cured him.

FAKE GHOST STORY

The night was dark and cold and a drizzling rain was falling. It was near midnight when Jack and Sue left a party at a friend's home. As they drove along the lonesome road, the engine sputtered and the car stopped. One look at the meter told Jack they were out of gas. He had forgotten to get some earlier in the evening and now here they were, miles from a gas station and not a building in sight except a dark, foreboding-looking house across the road.

Jack went up to the house and rang the doorbell. There was no answer. He tried the doorknob and the door opened. Thinking there might be a telephone inside, he stepped into the hallway. A heavy wind blew the door shut with a slam. In searching for the telephone, Jack fell over a chair and hit his head on a table, knocking him out.

Sue waited a while, and when Jack didn't reappear she tried the door, and she too entered the house. Thinking she heard Jack upstairs, she went to the second floor, using a tiny flashlight she had in her purse. Then she heard the shuffling of feet near her and called Jack's name, but there was no answer.

Now for the first time, Sue realized that she was in the famous haunted house. She screamed. Jack, regaining consciousness just in time to hear the scream, got to his feet and hurried upstairs to Sue. The shuffling feet kept coming, but neither Jack nor Sue could see anything. They kept backing away into the long hall. The shuffling feet kept coming, closer and closer. They finally bumped against a wall and knew that they were at the end of the hall. Now there seemed to be a group of shuffling feet. Closer and closer they came.

Jack fumbled around the wall and finally felt a doorknob. He opened the door and dragged Sue in with him. But he could not shut the door. Some unseen power seemed to hold it open. The shuffling feet seemed to be coming through the door. Jack and Sue backed away. Again a wall and again a doorknob. The door opened and they stepped through, only to find themselves trapped in a closet. The shuffling feet now seemed to fill the room. There seemed no hope.

Jack began to feel around for something with which to fight. Suddenly his hand touched a familiar instrument. "It's a drum," he whispered to Sue.

"That's great," shouted Sue. So they picked up the drum and beat it.

NOTE: These stories are from the original *Fun Encyclopedia* and are good for traveling stories, on rainy days, or around the campfire. Public libraries, bookstores, and various magazines are excellent resources for current stories, as well as folklore and favorites of yesteryear.

OTHER FUN

Mystery Trips—What fun it is to announce that the family is going on a Mystery Trip! But don't announce it too far in advance, or the children will drive you crazy trying to find out where you are going. Don't even give hints. Ideas for Mystery Trips:

1. The zoo
2. The local bakery (check to see when they are open to visitors)
3. A dairy farm to see cows milked, or a dairy to see the milk bottled
4. The museum
5. A television or radio station
6. The airport (have lunch while there)
7. A farm
8. The city market
9. A train ride if available
10. A bus ride in the city or to another town and back
11. Ballgames—high school, college, professional
12. The park—fly kites, hear a concert, picnic, feed ducks
13. A carnival or fair
14. Parades

15. Air shows
16. Pet shows
17. A cave
18. Historic sites
19. A shopping trip
20. Grandparents' house
21. An overnight camping trip
22. A week-end at a state park
23. The beach
24. The mountains
25. A lake

Vacation at Home—Many communities have tourist attractions that most local residents very seldom visit. Plan a vacation at home. Visit the tourist attractions near your community. Plan day trips to places nearby and return home at night. Go swimming, fishing, to the movies; play putt-putt golf, ride go-carts; visit museums, libraries, state parks; play in a water slide; sunbathe at the lake or in your backyard. Search the local papers for concerts in the parks or other attractions coming to your community. Schedule times to eat out—have breakfast in the park, go to a local restaurant for all your meals, or cook out every night.

Vacations are meant for rest and relaxation, but most of us return exhausted as well as broke. We could use the money spent for transportation, lodging, and meals on doing bigger and better things and having more fun at home. Reserve a room at the most plush motel in your community. Go to eat at places you normally could not afford. Be creative in your planning, but plan a vacation at home.

3

FUN WITH YOUNGER CHILDREN

There are many days when children ask for something to do. This chapter is loaded with suggestions.

A woman once said to an older adult who had a beautiful flower garden that she would love to grow flowers, but she didn't have time. When asked if she had children, the woman replied that she had three. The older adult told her that right now, she was growing the most important flowers—her children. There would be plenty of time later, when the children were grown and gone, to raise all the flowers she wanted.

Do not miss the joy of "growing" children into a responsible and happy adulthood. Children learn through play. You are the teacher, and we hope this book will help you discover new activities and rediscover those you cherished in your childhood. There are many suggestions in other volumes of *The New Fun Encyclopedia* that will help you enhance your time with your children. The bibliography in this volume also contains excellent resources.

As a family, you must find both quality and a quantity of time to be together. Don't neglect this key time in your lives.

Supplies—One of the important things to remember when growing children is to have on hand all kinds of "stuff" to grab and put into those hands that are actively looking for something to do. You might set aside a special closet or box where these supplies are kept readily available. Suggestions:

Paper:
Construction paper
Tissue paper
Crepe paper
White paper
Butcher paper (rolled up)
Newsprint
Paper bags
Newspapers
Magazines

Writing and Coloring Materials:
Crayons
Pencils
Felt-tip markers
Paint (caution)

Other Materials:
String
Colored stickers
Toothpicks
Q-sticks
Cotton balls
Egg cartons
Buttons
Pins
Scraps of cloth
Pieces of ribbon
Boxes of all sizes
Empty spools
Yarn
Scissors (blunt-end)
Cups (paper)

Adhesives:
Tape (Scotch and masking)
Glue and paste

Materials from the Kitchen:
Food coloring
Flour
Gelatin
Macaroni
  (elbow, alphabet)
Salt
Spaghetti
Starch
Sugar
Rice

When growing children, one must keep in mind several important factors: one's own childhood; advice from other parents; the words of educators and recreators; and good old common sense. Some basic principles were adequately stated by E. O. Harbin:

Children live in a world of play. The early Greeks recognized this, and therefore they built their educational system around the idea of play. Froebel recognized it when he initiated the kindergarten. Parents and other adults who deal with children must recognize it and be sympathetic toward the child's desire to play. Joseph Lee, in his *Play in Education,* insists that the grammar school, high school, and college, as well as the trade school, should make "deliberate provision for the development in every boy and girl of some form of expression" outside their expected occupation.

This volume cannot begin to hold all the innovative ideas born to mothers who dreamed up something new for a child to do. Here are but a few, which we hope will prove to be catalysts for your creative abilities.

FINGER PLAY

There are numerous kinds of finger plays. Here are some of the oldest and most familiar.

This Little Pig—Played with fingers or toes.

> This little pig went to market;
> This little pig stayed home;
> This little pig had roast beef;
> This little pig had none;
> This little pig said, "Wee, wee-e-e."

Ten Little Squirrels—Hold up all ten fingers, palms out. As each little squirrel is mentioned, the particular fingers on each hand are wiggled—the two thumbs, the two forefingers, the two second fingers, the two third fingers, and, for the fifth two squirrels—the brave ones—the two small fingers. On "Bang went the gun!" clap hands together suddenly. On "Away they run!" move hands out with the fingers wiggling.

> Ten little squirrels up in a tree.
> The first two said: "What's this we see?"
> The second two said: "A man with a gun!"
> The third two said: "Let's run! Let's run!"
> The fourth two said: "Let's hide in the shade."
> The fifth two said: "Shucks! We're not afraid!"
> Bang! went the gun! And away they run!

After saying this over once, children can do it with you. Try to include some dramatic touches—surprise, shock, fear, stealthiness, bravado.

Church and Steeple—

This is the church. (Palms down, interlock fingers on both hands.)

This is the steeple. (Straighten out the two forefingers, with the ends touching, to make the steeple.)

Open the door. (Pull thumbs back.)

And see the people. (Turn palms up, fingers intertwined and sticking up.)

FUN WITH PENCIL, PAPER, AND PAINT

Before people invented alphabets, they wrote their messages in pictures. Even today the apt illustration makes the written or printed word more vivid. Thus a child's response to pictures need cause no wonder. Sketching and painting, however crude, are an important part of your child's education. Encouraging children to draw some of their own ideas not only will afford a lot of fun but will help them become better acquainted with the world in which they live. Add color by furnishing crayons and paints, and you will enhance the value of this sort of creative play.

Johnny's Dog—*(Storyteller draws as the story is told.)*

Johnny lived in a house that looked like this. It had two windows and a door at the front. It had two chimneys, one on each side. Johnny had a dog, but he couldn't find him. So he said, "Maybe my dog is over at Sue's house." Now, Sue was Johnny's friend and she lived close by. Johnny had a special path that he followed to get to Sue's. So he started down this way, then turned sharply and went this way. He fell in a hole, but got up. He fell again. In fact, he fell four times. Then he came to a corner and started right up to Sue's house. *(All this time the storyteller has been drawing the route that Johnny followed.)* When he got there, smoke was coming out of the chimney. Johnny called to Sue and said, "Sue, have you seen my dog?"

"Yes, I have," Sue replied. "He has just gone home." So Johnny went straight home, and sure enough, there was his dog.

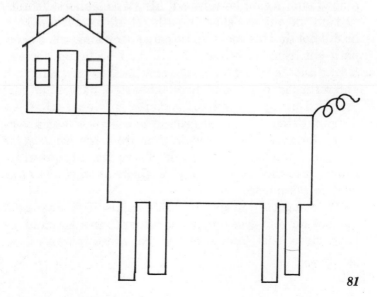

Fun with Younger Children

Johnny's Goose—*(Storyteller draws as story is told.)*

One day Johnny lost his goose. This dot represents
Johnny. *(Put a dot on the paper.)* Johnny lives in a little
round house. *(Draw a small circle around the dot.)* Near his
home is a pond. *(Draw a large oval.)* From Johnny's house
to the pond, there is a short path. *(Draw a line from the
small circle to the oval.)* Johnny went down the path and
looked around the pond for his goose. He went back in the
reeds but found no goose. He went back again four times in
different directions. Still no goose. Each time he retraced
his steps. *(Draw four lines at the end of the oval.)* Johnny
started back but decided to go way down from the
lake—way down. *(Draw a long line from the bottom of the
oval.)* But he came to a dead end. So he retraced his steps a
short distance and tried again. But he had no better luck.
(Draw a short branch out from the long path.) Again he
tried on the other side, but again he had no luck. *(Draw
another short line from the main path.)* So he went back to
the pond and started out on another path. *(Draw another
long line from the bottom of the oval.)* But again he came to
a dead end. Again he retraced his steps a short distance
and started out on a short bypath. *(Draw a short line.)* but
he did not find his goose, so he came back and took a short
path out from the other side. He had no better success.
(Draw another short line.) He went back to the main path
and returned to the pond. Brokenhearted, he went around
the pond and up the path to his house. He went to the front
door, but then he turned around and walked out a very
short distance. *(Draw a short line from the front of the
house.)* And what do you think? There was his goose! He
ran back to the house overjoyed. *(Draw another short line
back to the house.)*

"What a goose you are," he said to himself, "that you did
not look for your goose out front, rather than all around the
lake. Here it is!" And sure enough, there it was!

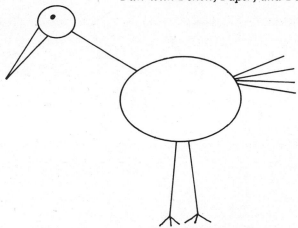

Creature—On a sheet of paper, make a couple of dots for eyes and a squiggly tail. Beginning with these few marks, your child can complete a drawing of a creature from the wild.

Spongy—Place an old sponge or rag in a small container of colored water, squeeze it gently to get out most of the water, and toss it several times on butcher paper. Your child can create a picture from this blob.

Double Drawing—Bind together two crayons, pencils, or felt-tip markers with a rubber band. Your child draws as usual, but the result is a double picture.

Blindfold Drawing—Blindfolded, let your child create a drawing, or assign a topic.

Rubbings—With the flat part of a crayon or a piece of charcoal, have your child rub across a sheet of onionskin paper placed on a flat object. Suggestions: leaves pressed flat; coins; flat, smooth rocks; smooth bark. Take the child(ren) to an old cemetery and rub over an old tombstone with charcoal or crayon on butcher paper.

Triangle Dots—Make dots on a piece of paper as illustrated. Players take turns connecting any two dots with a straight line. When a player can finish a triangle by adding a line, the player's initial is placed in the enclosed space. When all the dots have been connected, players' scores are indicated by the number of squares bearing their initial.

Tracing—With onionskin paper, your child can trace objects or pictures in magazines.

Letter Writing—Write a letter to the grandparents. If a child cannot write, print the words and let your child copy the letter. Have it dictated first, so that it will be in the child's own words.

Wiggles—This is a grand game for two players. It develops ingenuity and creativity, and gives expression to whatever artistic ability the player has. One does not need to be a skilled artist to get a lot of fun out of it.

One player draws a short wiggle line. The other player must make a drawing out of it. The paper may be turned sideways, upside down, or any way the artist desires. The result may be a house, a bird, an animal, a person, or anything the drawer pleases. When finished, the player should make the original wiggle part of the picture stand out heavier or blacker than the rest. If done at a party, players may be required to sign their creations. The various pictures may be placed on display.

Variation: Instead of a wiggle line, use a letter of the alphabet or a number as the beginning point for the drawing.

Funny Faces—Each player draws the funniest faces the imagination and the player's artistic ability will allow. If desired, bodies may be added. Suggestions may be offered regarding portraying certain moods—happy, glum, angry, surprised, frightened. Encourage children to use their own ideas in making their sketches. An example or two drawn by an adult may be helpful. Or a child and an adult may alternate in drawing faces. Examples:

Egg-head Sketching—Provide each child with a sheet of paper on which there are several egg-shaped ovals. Let them sketch faces in the ovals. Furnish crayons so that the pictures can be colored.

Eggshell Painting—This would be a fine activity for the Easter season. Instead of dyeing all the eggs, why not paint faces on some of them? The possibilities are limitless. And it is no end of fun. Use water colors or model paints.

Upside-down Face—Draw a face so that when turned upside down, it becomes another face.

Picture Letters—Letters that say most of what they have to say with pictures are fun for both the writer and the reader. Parents who write to their children will find their letters of more interest if they are illustrated with sketches. Theodore Roosevelt used to do this in the letters he wrote to the members of his family. One does not need to be an artist. The illustration here demonstrates one type of picture letter.

(Dear Tommy:

I will be home Sunday. I can hardly wait till then to see you. That's all for today!)

Finger Painting—Children can paint with their fingers, their hands, their arms, or their elbows. Spread out plenty of newspapers to protect the area. Or use oil cloth and wipe clean. Or paint in the bathtub.

1. Moisten an 18 × 24-inch sheet of highly glazed paper on both sides. Shelf paper is inexpensive, or waterpaint paper is available in most school supply stores.
2. Place the paint in metal pie pans or jar lids.
3. Cover the entire surface with paint, using the hand to spread the material.
4. Using the fingers, fist, forearm, sponge, jar lid, corrugated cardboard, potato or stick print—anything at hand—make a design or picture.
5. Let the painting dry on a smooth surface; then press it on the back with a hot iron to smooth out the wrinkles.
6. Spray it with neutral shellac to preserve it, if desired.

The Paint: Commercially made finger paint may be bought at most craft and hobby stores, or an inexpensive paint may be made from starch. Prepare the paste according to directions on the box. To each pint of paste add 1 tablespoon glycerine and ½ teaspoon oil of cloves. Wallpaper paste with enough water to make it the consistency of batter can be used in the same fashion. Kalsomine that has been mixed with hot water and allowed to jelly may also be used.

Color may be added in any of several ways: (a) food coloring may be added while the paste mixture is still warm (this method should be used if small children are to use the paint); (b) albastine or tempera may be powdered on dry or mixed with water and applied to the paper after the surface has been covered with paste; (c) drops of show-card paint may be placed on the paste-covered surface.

The paint comes off the hands easily with soap and warm water.

Mural—Hang a piece of butcher paper on the garage wall or some other place not easily marred. With paint and brush, let your children paint a mural (crayons will do just as well). The mural might be an interpretation of your family vacation, happy times with the family, a story about an animal, or a Bible story.

Collage—Have your children cut out pictures of food, animals, flowers, or families. (It would be best to stay with one subject, such as flowers.) Let them paste or glue these in a collage on a piece of poster board or heavy paper.

Animal Silhouettes—Provide each child with a pair of scissors, a sheet of white or dark paper, and a pencil. Call out the name of some animal—an elephant, for instance. Each child then draws and cuts out an elephant. Next a dog, or a cat, or any other animal may be silhouetted. Animals cut out of white paper can be pasted on a dark background; those cut out of dark paper, on a white background.

Make a Chain—(This could be for the Christmas tree.) Have available construction paper in a variety of colors or, if for a Christmas tree, red and green. Cut the paper into 3 X 1-inch strips. Form one strip into a loop and glue or staple the ends together. Loop a second strip inside the first and fasten the ends of the second together. Continue in this way until all the strips have been used or until the chain is as long as desired.

Placemats—For each placemat, you will need two sheets of different colored construction paper. In one sheet, cut slits widthwise, one inch apart and to within one inch of each edge. Cut the other sheet into one-inch strips, widthwise. Weave these strips through the slits in the other sheet, and you'll have a placemat. Make several for the family for a special Family Night at Home.

Lantern—Fold a piece of colored construction paper lengthwise. Starting at the fold, cut slits one inch apart, to within an inch from the edges. Unfold the paper and tape the short edges together. Set it on end and press slightly, and you'll obtain a lantern effect. Add another strip to the top for a handle. This can be another Family Night at Home decoration made by the children.

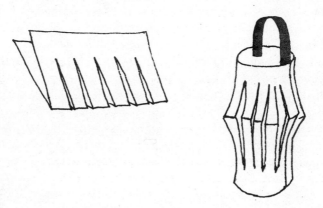

Paper Tree—To make a paper tree, cut two double pages of the comic section of a newspaper in two, parallel with the top of the page. This will give you four pieces, each half the width of the paper and two widths long.

Roll up one piece lengthwise, three-fourths of the way, with space in the center large enough to place two fingers. Slip in another piece on top of the one-fourth of the first piece not rolled and continue to roll. Start the third piece and the fourth piece in the same manner.

Now cut four slits down from one end, about halfway. The best way is to cut down once, then cut just across from that cut, then cut equidistant between those cuts.

Then grasp the center piece on the cut end and pull up.

Jacob's Ladder—Jacob's Ladder is made from the same number of papers as the paper tree. Cut the papers across the same way into four strips, each half the width of the paper and two widths long.

Now fold one end of the first piece over to the first crease, or to the middle of the strip. Fold this over three more times and the folded part will be about three-fourths of an inch wide. Then roll, with this folded part in the center, just as for the tree, keeping the hole in the center about large enough for your two fingers. Continue rolling in the other strips of paper.

Then put a round stick in the center of the roll, with the folded part of the paper underneath this stick. With a sharp knife, cut through the paper above the stick in two places, dividing the paper into thirds. Cut through to the stick and down the sides, being careful not to cut through to the folds. Take out the stick and break the ends of the paper over so that the top part is cut down the sides, and the bottom part is only slightly wider than the folds.

Then with scissors, cut across the center piece of the three parts, parallel with the roll.

Now grasp the top fold with one hand, hold the other two ends with the other hand, and pull the ladder out to its full length.

Draw Me—Have your child stretch out on butcher paper or newspaper. Then outline his or her body. Let your child fill in the outline, drawing the face and clothing and coloring eyes, hair, and so on.

Variation: Draw an outline of your child's hand or foot for a keepsake.

FUN WITH PAPER BAGS

Make Masks—Cut the bag off to about shoulder length or a little longer. Then cut places for eyes, nose, and mouth, and let your child decorate the mask as desired. Different shapes can be glued on the mask to make it more scary, or it can be crayoned or painted.

Make Clothes (costumes)—Cut out armholes and a place for the head to go through the bottom of the bag. Let your child decorate this new armor.

Make Boots—Select bags that fit your child's feet. Tie with a string around the ankle, or use a rubber band.

Make a Vest—Cut armholes and a hole in the bottom of the bag for the head to go through. Then cut up the middle of the bag so it will open like a vest. Your child can decorate it as an Indian or cowboy vest.

Make a Puppet—Use a small bag—one that will fit the hand of your child. Children can design their own puppets, perhaps create special characters. A child places a hand in a bag and makes the puppet act out a story.

Make Hats—Find a bag that will not slip down over your child's face. Fold the top of the bag several times to strengthen the base of the hat. Cut, shape, color, or glue on designs to make a hat, crown, or helmet.

OTHER IDEAS

Play Dough—Give your child some play dough and a cookie cutter, or just let the child's imagination take over. Play dough can be purchased, or it can be made at home.

PLAY DOUGH RECIPE

1 cup flour	2 tsp. cream of tartar
½ cup salt	1 T. cooking oil
1 cup water	

Mix all ingredients. Cook over medium heat, stirring constantly. When mixture forms a doughy lump, pour out onto the table and knead. Store in an airtight container.

Egg Hunt—Real or candy eggs can be hidden. Children can gather the eggs in paper sacks or tiny baskets. Extra points may be allowed (if points are used) for a gold or silver egg. Children should be encouraged to share with others who do not find many eggs.

Variation: Peanuts may be hidden in the same manner. It adds to the fun if the children are divided into groups and given names of animals or fowls. In this case, the children cannot pick up the peanuts. A "cat" mews when a cache of peanuts is discovered, and the "keeper" comes running to pick up the treasure. The "dogs" bark, the "ducks" quack, and the "sheep" baa-aa-aa.

Make Bowing Dolls—Straighten a hairpin. Bend one end until it resembles a shepherd's crook. Fix several of these pins. Then look through magazines until you find just the pictures you want—men, women, or animals of a size just a little longer than the pins.

Thrust the hairpins through these paper dolls and hang the bent edges of the pins over a table edge. The hairpin will swing back and forth like a pendulum. Blow slightly on these dolls and watch them bow politely, bobbing back and forth in amusing fashion.

These tiny actors will make a great deal of fun for children.

Blow Bubbles—You need only a large bowl of soapy water and some clay pipes or regular soap blowing pipes. Add a little glycerine to give the bubbles a prismatic effect.

Try Bean Art—Supply a piece of heavy cardboard or construction paper, some dried beans, and some glue, and let your child design an artistic creation. Beans of several different colors will enhance this art work.

Read a Book to Your Child—It is well for a family to invest early in excellent books that will help a child grow and develop. Christian bookstores offer an excellent variety of books for children, as do other reputable bookstores. Visit your community library often and let your child become familiar with it and with the librarian. Good reading habits begin in early childhood.

Make a Scrapbook—Help your child start a scrapbook. There are so many ideas for scrapbooks that your imagination can run wild. Suggestions:

Airplanes	Space flights and vehicles
Birds	Cars
Boats	Historical data
A current President	Dogs and cats
Other animals	Kindergarten work
Vacations	Sports

Start a Collection—Even very young children enjoy collecting things. Some collections begun as a child can become lifetime hobbies. Suggestions:

Series of books	Matchbook covers
Stamps	Thimbles
Autographs	Miniature glass
Postcards	Bells
Rocks	Earrings
Jewelry	Coins (foreign, domestic)
Belt buckles	Bottles

Make Models—Some of us often do not take time to help our children work with their hands, and they frequently fail to develop this skill. Very simple to very complex models can be purchased at most toy or department stores.

Fly Kites—In a windy season, go fly kites.

Have a Closet Search—Let your children go to the storage room or attic, take out the old clothes, and play act.

Go for a Walk—Discover the neighborhood and meet new friends. See what other people have done to their yards and gardens.

Teach Games—It is good to teach children how to play with one another in fun activities. In this century, we are privileged also to have many learning games in the field of electronics. Visit stores that offer these games and discover those that are best suited for your children. Table games from various companies are still favorites. Be wise in your selection of table games, card games, video games, and just good old fun games. Many suitable for younger children can be found in chapter 4.

4

FUN WITH CHILDREN'S GAMES

This section of the book is filled with games for children. Some games call for several players, so invite the neighborhood children to join in. Read carefully to see if a game will apply to the age of your child or children. Some of the games are a little strenuous, but with proper supervision, they should be fun. Here are E. O. Harbin's timeless suggestions for instructing children in games.

1. Get attention before explaining the game. Don't try to shout directions above the noise of the group. Speak in a normal tone. To obtain quiet, adopt some method that works for you. Different people use different techniques. Some can get attention simply by standing quietly before the group. Some use the lifted hand, with the children, one by one, lifting their hands as they observe the other lifted hands.
2. Appeal to the imagination. Children are always responsive to the imaginative touch. A ball can become a fox or a rabbit. A handkerchief can become a snake with the greatest of ease. You should see the eyes of seven-year-olds sparkle as they play Dwarf Hide-and-Go-Seek!
3. Get into position to play a new game before explaining it. The explanation becomes more intelligible then.

4. Do more demonstrating than talking. Children want action.
5. Do not try to teach a game you do not know well.
6. Have all necessary equipment ready before beginning.
7. Use children as leaders whenever possible. Encourage them to share their knowledge of games.
8. Do not permit certain aggressive children to monopolize a game.
9. Once rules are established, see that they are observed. Build up a healthy respect for their observance.
10. Enjoy playing. Children are quick to sense a leader's "This-is-a-pain-to-me" attitude.

COUNTING OUT

1—Eeny, meeny, miny, mo,
Cracka, feeny, finy, fo,
Mamma woocha, papa doocha,
Rick, bick, ban, do.

2—Eeny, meeny, miny, mo,
Catch a bad boy by his toe;
If he hollers make him pay
Fifty dollars every day.

3—Wire, brier, limberlock!
Three geese in a flock!
One flew east. One flew west.
And one flew over the cuckoo's nest.
O-U-T spells out,
And out go you.

4—One, two, three, four, five!
I caught a hare alive.
Six, seven, eight, nine, ten!
I let him go again.

5—Eenie, meenie, dixie, deenie,
Hit 'em a lick and John McQueenie,
Time, time, American time,
Eighteen hundred and ninety-nine.
O-U-T spells out,
And out you go.

6—Hic-up, snick-up,
Isaac, Jacob,
Two-cup, penny-cup,
Good for the hic-ups.
O-U-T spells out,
And out you go.

7—Apples, peaches, pears, and plums,
Tell me when your birthday comes.
[Tell the date of birthday of person "comes" comes out
on, then count out that number. Example: October
12—count to 12.]
And out you go.

8—[Children hold out both fists, then count around.]
One potato, two potato,
Three potato, four,
Five potato, six potato,
Seven potato more.
[The fist "more" comes out on goes behind the back.
When both fists are behind the back, step out of
counting. Last fist out is IT.]

GUESSING GAMES

Cricket—Players sit in a circle. Provide one player with a metal cricket, such as used by drillmasters. One player, chosen as a Frog, stands inside the circle. The cricket is passed around the circle, the players trying to hide its location from the Frog. The holder of the cricket watches an opportunity to snap it when the Frog is not looking, and then hastily passes it on to another player. If the Frog finds the cricket, the player who had it becomes the Frog.

Crambo—One player begins the game by saying, for instance, "I am thinking of something in this room that rhymes with *fair*." The others ask, "Is it chair?" "Is it hair?" "Is it pear?" and so on until they guess it. The one who guesses correctly starts another. The game may be varied by enlarging the boundaries so that thoughts are not confined to the room. Or the limits may be determined by some classification such as nature lore, geography, etc.

I Spy—One player leaves the room. The rest hide an object in plain sight, but in an unusual place. The child returns to the room and tries to find the hidden article, which may be a knife, an eraser, a ball, a book, etc.
Variations:
(a) More than one player may be sent out. As the players find the article they sit down, but do not disclose the hiding place to the others. So it goes until all players are seated.
(b) Hide the object out of sight. The children who know where the object is hidden help the searcher by saying, "Cold," "Warmer," "Very warm," "Hot," etc. When the hunter is far away from the object, they say, "Cold." When very close, they say "Hot," or "Red hot."

Who Is Knocking?—Children sit quietly. One child is chosen to sit on a stool in the front of the room, with eyes tightly closed and hands held over them.

Another child goes up and knocks on the floor behind the player on the stool.

"Who is knocking at my door?" calls the child with the closed eyes.

"It is I," the child who knocked must answer immediately, though the voice may be disguised.

The child on the stool has three guesses to discover who knocked. If the child guesses correctly, the two players exchange places and another knocker is selected.

Animal Blind Man's Bluff—One player, blindfolded and holding a stick or cane, stands in the center of a circle of players. The other players dance around in the circle until the "blind man" taps on the floor. At that signal they must stand still. The "blind man" then points the cane at some player. That player must take the other end of the cane. The "blind man" commands the player to make a noise like some animal—a cow, cat, dog, lion, donkey, goat, duck, parrot, hog. The "blind man" then tries to guess who the player is. If the guess is correct, they exchange places. If not, the game proceeds, the "blind man" trying again with some other player.

Players may disguise their voices, thereby making some peculiar animal sounds. They may also disguise their height by stooping or standing on tiptoe before answering.

Imaginative Hunting—This is mental hide-and-go-seek. One player decides on a place of hiding. Bounds have been set by common agreement, such as "in the house," "in the room," "in the yard." "Guess where I am hiding." The player who guesses has the privilege of hiding next time. If the bounds are confined to the room, the player may hide in a vase, in a desk drawer, behind a flower pot, etc., since this is an imaginative game.

Geography Hide-and-Go-Seek—Use a map. "I am thinking of a river in Brazil. It begins with an *A*." Of course that's *Amazon*, and the player guessing it must not only name it, but must locate it on the map. "I am thinking of the capital of Kentucky." The guesser must locate Frankfort on the map. If one of those large picture maps is available, such questions as "I am thinking of a state that has the most wheat (or corn, or cattle, or cotton, etc.)" would be a simple way for children to pick up some geography.

Hidden Object—"Guess what object in this room I am thinking of. It begins with the letter —."

Nature Hunting—"Guess what tree I am thinking of." "Guess what bird." "Guess what animal." "Guess what insect." Cues may be given to help the group locate the particular subject. For instance, the hider may say, "The bird I have in mind has a red stripe on a black wing. It is often seen on swaying cattails in swampy land."

Button, Button, Who's Got the Button?—Players sit or stand in a circle with one player at the center. In the circle of players is a button which the players pass back and forth. All players keep their hands in constant motion as if they are receiving or passing the button. The center player tries to guess who has the button. When the guess is correct, players change places.
Variation: Pass a thimble or coin.

Circus—Sides are chosen and the two leaders sit facing each other, the members of each side sitting as close to their respective leaders as possible.
One leader begins by mentioning an animal whose name begins with the letter *A*, and then counts to ten (not too fast). Before that leader has finished counting, the other

leader must mention another animal beginning with the same letter, and so on until neither can think of any more animals whose names begin with *A.* Then they start with *B,* then with *C,* etc.

The sole duty of the other players is to think of new names and suggest them to their leaders.

If either side fails to give a name before the ten count has expired, the opposing side has a choice from among their number.

The Toy Shop—One child acts as shopkeeper. Another, the customer, goes out of the room. The rest of the children decide what toys they will be, each child representing one toy. The customer comes in and asks for certain toys. If the customer asks for a top, the person who is a "top" spins around. If a bugle, the "bugle" blows, imitating the sound of the instrument. Thus it goes—the "doll" walks stiffly and says, "Ma-ma!"; the "violin" plays; the "scooter" scoots; the "skates" skate; the "football" runs signals or kicks.

Woman from the Wood—Players are divided into two equal groups. The two lines face each other. One line advances toward the other, saying, "Here comes the woman from the wood." The second line answers, "What can you do?" The first line responds, "Anything!" The second line then says, "Work away!" The players of the first line now imitate some occupation in which the woman might engage. They have previously agreed among themselves as to what this shall be. So they iron, or wash, or sweep, or churn, or sew, or dig in the garden, or pull weeds, or pick flowers, or knead dough, or stir cake, or whip cream, or knit, or phone. The other side tries to guess what is being done. If they guess correctly, they become the woman. If not, the first line tries again.

Third Degree—Players are divided into two equal groups and go to different rooms. Or if outdoors, they are separated by some distance. Each group selects one of its own number to represent them. The two players selected get together outside and decide on some object—a tree, a chair, a piano, a book, a flower, a vase, a chandelier, etc. Each goes now to the opposite group. The idea is to see which side can first guess the object decided upon by means of questions that can be answered yes or no. The side that first guesses correctly keeps the player who came to them and, in addition, gets its own member back. Two more players are chosen and the game continues.

Hunt the Key—A key is placed on a long piece of twine, and the ends of the twine are tied together. The players form a circle, all holding the twine and keeping their hands constantly in motion. One player stands inside the circle and tries to discover where the key is. A player caught with the key becomes IT.

Mother Goose Quiz—Someone starts this game by asking a question about a Mother Goose rhyme. For instance, if the question is, "Who stole a pig?" the first player to shout "Tom, Tom, the piper's son" is allowed to quote that rhyme and then is permitted to ask the next question. However, if the player cannot quote the rhyme, the one who does may be allowed to ask the question.

Blind Neighbors—Half the players have paper bags over their heads so that they cannot see. The chair to the right of each "blind" player is vacant. The other players sit in these chairs and perform in various ways. For instance, they say "Howdy!" "Hello!" crow like a rooster, quack like a duck, sneeze, cough, sing, bleat like a sheep, etc. As soon as a blindfolded player recognizes the person in the chair, the paper bag may be removed.

Dwarf Hide-and-Go-Seek—In their imaginations the players may make themselves as small as they desire—a half-inch tall, three inches, six inches. They then hide in or behind anything in the room—a vase, a thimble, a hat, a book, a picture, etc. One youngster hid up his daddy's sleeve. The one who is IT tries to discover where the "dwarf" is hidden. If the hunter is having trouble, the hider may give some cues, such as, "I am hidden on that side of the room." This is a grand game for a parent and an imaginative child. If you have recently been reading *Gulliver's Travels,* you could imagine you are Lilliputians when you are hiding and that you are Gulliver when you are hunting.

Sniping—Two blankets or sheets are required for this game. The players are divided into two equal sides. Each side selects a player to be hidden. Two teammates then hold the blanket so that the player chosen is hidden from the player chosen by the other side. Each player tries to find out who is behind the other blanket, without being discovered. They may push each other and chase each other, but neither is allowed to touch the other with the hands. The first player to guess who the other player is scores a point. Two other players are then chosen.

Who Has Gone?—Children stand or sit in a circle. One player, IT, puts hands over closed eyes. Then another player quietly leaves the room. The player who is IT, with eyes open, then tries to guess which child is gone. If the guess is correct, the player who went out becomes IT. If not, the game continues until IT does guess correctly.

Huckle, Buckle—One group of players leaves the room. The rest hide some object, leaving it in plain sight but where it will not be easily seen—for instance, on top of a picture, in a corner of the room, behind a vase. After the object has been hidden the players who went out are recalled. They begin the hunt. A player who discovers the object sits down immediately, saying "Huckle, buckle, bean stalk!" but tries not to tip off the other hunters as to the location of the object. The hunt continues until all players have found the object. Then the player who first found it has the privilege of hiding it as a new group of players is sent out of the room.

Who Has the Ring?—Players stand or sit in a circle or straight line. One player has a ring. The other players hold their hands clasped in front of them. The player with the ring goes from player to player, tapping their closed fists as if putting the ring in their possession. The ring may actually have been given to the first person, but the player goes to each in turn, pretending to deposit the ring and saying to each:

> Biddy, Buddy, hold fast my gold ring,
> Till I go to London and come back again.

Each child in turn is called on by the leader to guess who has the ring. If successful, the child takes the leader's place.

ACTIVE GAMES

Hopscotch—This is an old game that gives good practice in body balance and agility. Any one of a variety of diagrams is marked on the ground or walk. Not more than three or four should play on one diagram or there will be too long a wait between turns.

A player stands on both feet, two or three feet from the base of the diagram, and tosses a small flat stone, trying to get it in space Number 1. If successful, player hops on one foot into space Number 1, picks up the rock, still standing on one foot, and hops out. Player next throws the stone for

Number 2, hops into Number 1, then into Number 2, picks up the stone, hops back into Number 1, and out. This continues until player fails: when stone does not land in the correct space or lands on a line, when player's foot touches a line, when player fails to pick up stone, or when the other foot or a hand touches the ground. Once player has hopped into a space, foot must remain stationary until player hops into next space.

When using a diagram similar to B, when player reaches Numbers 2/3, 5/6, and 8/9, both feet are used, one in each square, unless the stone is in one of those squares.

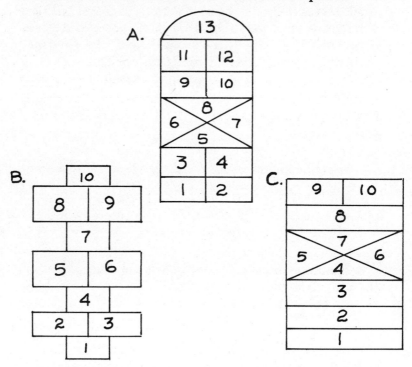

Hickory, Dickory, Dock—Small children enjoy going through the simple movements of this game. They recite the nursery rhyme as they act out the words.

Hickory, dickory, dock,
[Move arms to right, then left, pendulum fashion.
Stamp foot.]
The mouse ran up the clock.
[Run four steps forward.]
The clock struck One!
[Pause a moment to listen, hand to ear. On "One!" clap hands.]
And down it run.
[Run four steps back to place.]
Hickory, dickory, dock.
[Move arms to right, then left, pendulum fashion.
Stamp foot.]

Jack Be Nimble—Place an eight- to ten-inch-tall object upright on the floor to represent a candlestick. Players run in single file and jump with both feet over the candlestick, while reciting:

> Jack be nimble,
> Jack be quick,
> Jack jump over the candlestick.

All the action is in rhythm. Players try to avoid knocking over the candlestick.

Seesaw Marjorie Daw—This simple game adds drama to the fun of the rhythm.

Seesaw, Marjorie Daw,
[Raise arms sideward. Sway body to left and right.]
Jack shall have a new master.
[Partners join hands. Skip forward four steps.]
He shall have but a penny a day,
[Step left. Point right toe forward, shaking right forefinger at partner, left hand on hip.]

Because he won't work any faster.
[Join both hands with partner. Skip around in place four
steps.]

Bogeyman—One player, the Bogeyman, stands at one
goal. The other players are lined up at the opposite goal.
The Bogeyman steps out and shouts, "Are you afraid of the
Bogeyman?" At this the other players run toward the
Bogeyman's goal, and the Bogeyman tries to tag them.
Players caught must go with the Bogeyman to the opposite
goal to act as aids in catching the rest of the runners. The
last player caught becomes the new Bogeyman. Or it may
be decided that the first one caught should be IT.

Ringmaster—One child is chosen for ringmaster. If the
child can flourish a whip like a real circus ringmaster, it
will increase interest. The other players form a circle
around the ringmaster without holding hands.

The ringmaster moves around inside the circle, snap-
ping the whip, and calls the name of some animal. The
players in the circle immediately imitate the animal's
movements and cries. For instance, for an elephant, they
would droop their shoulders, stoop over, and walk
swinging their hands like a trunk. For a bear, they would
run on all fours and growl, or stand and claw. For a frog,
they would hop and croak. Other animals could be a
barking dog, a mewing or purring cat, a humped and
swaying camel, a snarling and springing tiger, a roaring
and nervous lion, a balking and braying donkey, a
scratching and cackling hen, a mooing cow, a neighing and
galloping horse, a crowing rooster, etc.

The ringmaster may announce, "All join the circus
parade!" At this, each player chooses some animal to
represent and gallops around the circle with suitable
movements.

High Windows—All the players but one join hands in a circle. IT stands inside the circle. Passing around, IT tags one of the players in the circle. Then they both run around the outside of the circle, the vacant place being left open. The player who was tagged tries to tag IT before they go around the circle three times. If the chaser fails to tag IT the other players call "High window!" and raise their clasped hands to let both players inside. The chaser then becomes IT, and the game continues.

Singing Tag—This starts the same as ordinary tag, with IT chasing the runners. However, if IT is very fleet of foot, a person about to be tagged may burst into song. As long as players keep singing, they may not be tagged. Once they stop, however, IT may tag them and then they must join IT in chasing the runners. If a player bursts into laughter instead of song, the player may be tagged. Grown-ups can play this singing tag, too.

Washer Line-toss—A line is drawn about ten feet away from the players. Each player has a washer. In turn they toss these washers at the line. The one who lands closest to the line scores a point. Players may slide the washer or toss it through the air. Ten points may constitute a game. If played on the sidewalk, the crack between slabs may serve as the line.

Here I Bake—Players join hands in a circle. One player inside the circle is the captive and endeavors to find freedom by trickery and force. Touching one pair of clasped hands, the captive says, "Here I bake!" Passing around the circle, the captive touches another pair of hands, saying, "Here I brew!" Suddenly, in a place least suspected, the prisoner whirls around, springs at two clasped hands, and tries to break through, shouting, "Here I mean to break through!" The prisoner endeavors to catch two players off guard. The two players responsible for the prisoner's escape draw straws to determine which takes the prisoner's place.

Flowers and the Wind—This game is suitable for small children. The players are divided into two equal teams, each team having a home marked off at opposite ends of the playground, with a long neutral space between. One team represents a flower, deciding among themselves which flower they shall represent—daisies, lilies, lilacs, etc. They then walk over near the home line of the opposite team. The opposite players (who represent the wind) stand in a row on their line, ready to run. They try to guess the flower chosen by their opponents. As soon as the right flower is named, the entire flower team must turn and run home, the wind team chasing them. Any players caught by the wind before reaching home become their prisoners and join them. The remaining flowers repeat their play, taking the name of a different flower each time. This continues until all the flowers have been caught.

Bow-wow—The players form a large circle. One player, IT, runs around outside the circle. IT suddenly taps some player in the circle and keeps on going. The tapped player immediately begins to run the opposite way around the circle. When the two players meet, they must go down on all fours and say "Bow-wow!" three times. Then each goes on around the circle, trying to reach the vacated place first. The one left out is IT the next time.

Driving Piggy to Market—Each contestant or team will need a pop bottle, a milk carton, or a can, and a stick. An umbrella or cane will do for the stick.

At the signal, each contestant begins to push the "pig" toward a designated goal, then brings it back in the same manner. The player is allowed to use only one hand, holding the other behind the back.

If done as a relay, the two teams line up single file. As soon as a player gets the "pig" back home, the next player drives it to market and back.

It will be found that the "pig" is not always easy to control.

Air Route—The players are seated, preferably in a circle. Each is given the name of some city or airport or country. One player, IT, has no chair. IT stands inside the circle and calls, "All aboard for the plane from Oklahoma City to Boston! All aboard!" The two players representing Oklahoma City and Boston must change seats, and IT tries to get a seat in the scramble. The player left out becomes IT, and the game continues.

Falling in the Lake—This game may be played with or without chairs. A space six to eight feet wide is marked off on the floor for a lake. If chairs are used, they are placed in a circle, facing out. The players march around the circle to music. When the music stops all marchers must stop where they are. If players are in the space marked off as the lake, they are considered to have fallen into the lake and are out of the game. They take seats in the chairs. All players are required to walk through the lake, and all players must stay in line. In a large group there may be more than one lake. The game may be continued until only one player is left.

Crab Race—The children go down on all fours. In this position they move backward toward the goal line.

Variation: **Crab and Monkey Relay**—The race may be run as a relay, in which case all players on a team would be lined up single file behind the starting line, and the players may come back as monkeys. That is, they face forward.

Bag Tag—One player has a big paper bag with the mouth folded back several times to make it easier to handle. Suddenly the player with the bag claps it over the head of another player so that it covers the entire head and the player, IT, cannot see. All the other players scatter. IT counts, "One, two, three! Stop!" and immediately, all players must stop where they are. IT then moves about hands out, until some player is touched. IT asks this player to imitate some animal. The captured player must answer appropriately, in a disguised voice, of course. If IT correctly identifies the captured player, the bag is placed on that person's head, and the group scatters again. If the guess is incorrect, IT keeps trying.

Hit 'em Tag—In this game, a soft rag ball, a tennis ball, a sponge ball, or a small play ball is used. One player is IT. The rest scatter as IT tries to hit one of them with the ball. If IT misses, the player nearest the ball picks it up and tosses it back. IT keeps trying until someone is hit.

Black Hole—One player is IT. The others choose trees or posts or large rocks as their spaceports. IT marks off on the ground as many Black Holes as there are players. The children run out from their spaceports and IT pursues them. When IT catches a player, that child is put in one of the Black Holes. A captured player may be freed by being touched by one of the other players. After being freed a player may return to his or her spaceport unmolested. The person who freed the player, however, may be caught by IT. When all the players are caught, a new IT is selected.

Pirate's Cave—One player is the Pirate, who hides behind a bush, tree, or chair. Another player is the mother or father. The rest are children. The children call to their parent:

Mother (Father), may we go out
If we behave?

The parent answers:

Yes, but don't go near
The Pirate's cave!"

The children then leave home base and walk or run around until the parent shouts: "Children, come home!"

At this signal the Pirate leaves the hiding place and starts in pursuit of the children, growling fiercely. The children run for home base, screaming as if frightened.

All the children the Pirate tags must join the Pirate to help catch the others next time.

Cowboys and Indians—The players are divided into two even sides. The cowboys are supposed to be camped in the woods. They fall asleep, leaving one player to stand guard. The Indians are hidden in the bushes, behind trees, etc. They come from their hiding places and approach the cowboys. If they can tag some cowboys before they get up, the cowboys are captured. However, they are not likely to be able to do this, for the watchman will sound the alarm. The cowboys then get up and rush after the Indians before they can get back to their "wigwams." Captured Indians become cowboys. The Indians may then be allowed to go to sleep while the cowboys slip up on them.

Pretty Girls' Station—This old game is variously called **Lemonade, New York Town, New Orleans, Sugar-loaf Town,** and **Georgia Town.** The players are divided into two even sides. Boundaries are decided. One group approaches the other, each group having its players arranged in a straight line. The following dialogue takes place:

"Here we come!"
"Where from?"

"Pretty Girls' Station!"
"What's your trade?"
"Lemonade!"
"How's it made?" *or* "Go to work!"

Immediately the players who have approached go through motions that represent some activity—sweeping, picking cotton, churning, washing clothes, ironing, sewing, driving nails, etc. As soon as the opposing side guesses correctly, the pantomimers must dash back to their own goal line with the guessers in pursuit. All players tagged go over to the other side and the game continues, with the other side pantomiming.

Variation: Instead of chasing and running, points may be allowed for a correct guess.

Loo K'bah Zee—This is a game played by boys in far-off Burma. One boy holds a stone or other small object and walks up and down behind the other players, who stand in a row with their hands held open behind them. As he walks up and down, he pretends to put the stone in various hands. Finally he drops the object in someone's hands, and that player runs out of the line, trying to avoid being caught by the boys on either side of him. They may not move out of their places, but must catch him as he leaves. If he is caught, he changes places with the boy behind the row. If he is not caught, he goes back to his own place and the play continues, the first boy behind the line continuing to walk up and down, depositing the stone in someone's hands, until a boy is caught to take his place.

King of the Mountain (King of the Castle)—One player is chosen by lot to be King and assumes a position on a mound of earth or on a large rock. The player must protect his or her right to this position, however.

Fair pulls and pushes are allowed, but players are not permitted to grab the King's clothes. Penalty for such a foul is to be set aside as a prisoner of war—virtual expulsion from the game.

The King may have an ally who notes fouls and expels those who commit them. The ally, therefore, is nothing more than a referee.

The chances for the King to retain the Mountain for long are not good. The player who succeeds in getting the King off the mountain becomes King for the next game.

Sling the Statue—One player is the Slinger. The Slinger takes other players by the hand, slings them around, and lets go. A player who is slung is off balance and must remain frozen in the position that results when his or her motion stops. This makes for some funny statues. Players take turns as the slinger.

The Sea—Players are seated in a circle, facing out, except one, who represents the Sea. That player stands outside the circle. Each person is given the name of some denizen of the sea—whale, shark, porpoise, star, sail, sword, buffalo, perch, cat, etc. The Sea walks slowly around outside the ring, calling one fish after another to follow. Whan all the fish, or a goodly number of them, have left their seats, the Sea begins to run about, exclaiming, "The Sea is troubled! The Sea is troubled!" Suddenly the Sea sits down in one of the chairs. All "fish" follow the Sea's example as long as seats are available. The player left out becomes the Sea and the game continues.

Letting Out the Doves—Players stand in groups of three. One in each group, usually the smallest, represents a dove. Another, a hawk, is larger or swifter than the dove. The third player is the owner of the birds.

The dove stands in front of the owner and holds the owner's hand. The hawk stands behind the owner and is also held by the hand.

The owner throws the dove with a gesture of the hand, as a bird might be tossed for flight in the air. The dove sails away, arms extended like wings. When the dove has a sufficient start so that the hawk may not catch the player too easily, the owner throws the hawk in the same fashion. The hawk, too, runs with extended arms as though flying and tries to catch the dove. The hawk must run over exactly the same route as the dove. When the owner claps hands or gives some other signal for the birds to return, the dove tries to get back without being caught by the hawk. The clapping is usually done with hollow hands to make a deep sound. This signal is usually given when the dove reaches the farthest point to which the owner thinks it best to go. The dove may not come home until the signal is given.

Master of the Ring—A circle is drawn on the ground. Players stand shoulder to shoulder inside the circle with arms folded, either on their chests or behind their backs. At the signal, players try to push one another out of the circle. A player who steps on the circle, unfolds the arms, or falls down is out. The last player standing is Master of the Ring.

Birdcage Tag—All the "birds" are in a "nest" at one side of the playing space. The nest is a space marked off in some way on the ground or floor. The "cage" is on the other side of the playing space, marked off in similar fashion. Both cage and nest are at the end of a baseline. One player, the Hawk, stands between the nest and the cage.

The players are divided into groups. Each group selects the kind of bird it will represent and tells the "bird keeper." The bird keeper tells the Hawk what birds are in the nest—robins, redbirds, bluebirds, sparrows, etc.

The Hawk calls to the bird keeper, "I want a bluebird." The bird keeper calls, "Bluebirds, fly, but don't let the Hawk catch you."

Immediately all the bluebirds must leave the nest and run across to the opposite side. The Hawk tries to catch them. Those caught must go to the space marked off for the cage. The birds are safe when they cross the opposite base line. The Hawk then calls for another bird—the robin, for instance. This continues until all the birds are caught. In a large group there may be two or more Hawks.

Blind Man's Bluff Catch—A blindfolded player is led to the center of the room, taken by the shoulders, and turned about three times. The blindfolded player then tries to catch and identify one of the other players. In a large space, limits will have to be set, beyond which the players may not go to avoid being caught.

Washer Woman—Players stand in couples, in two lines, facing one another. Couples clasp adjacent hands. They slowly swing their arms three times toward the right, then three times toward the left. As they do this, they sing:

This is the way we wash our clothes,
wash our clothes, wash our clothes.

Then they unclasp their hands and rub them together as if washing clothes, singing:

This is the way we rub our clothes,
rub our clothes, rub our clothes.

Now the couples again clasp hands. The line on one side stands with arms raised, and the couples on that side slip through the other line so that the two lines stand back to back. Immediately the other side repeats the movement so that the couples are again face to face. This is done quickly, three times in succession, while the players sing:

This is the way we wring our clothes,
wring our clothes, wring our clothes,

Then suddenly they stop and clap their hands, singing:

And hang them on the bushes.

Hide and Seek—While one player, IT, with eyes hidden at home base, counts to twenty, the other children hide. Then IT shouts, "Here I come, ready or not!" and begins to look for the other players. Upon spying a hider, IT calls, "One two three on ———," and both hider and seeker race back to base. If IT reaches base first, the hider is "out." A hider who reaches base first shouts, "Home free!" A hider may also sneak home while IT is too far from base to race back. The first person "out" becomes IT for the next game. If IT is unable to find all the hiders, or if the game must stop before all hiders are caught, IT calls, "Allee allee outs in free!"

Frog in the Middle—Players form a circle. One player is the frog and sits at the center. The other players crowd around and tease the frog, but try to keep from being tagged. The frog is not permited to move from his position in the center of the floor. If the frog can tag a player, that player becomes IT. The children may taunt the frog, calling "Frog in the middle, can't catch me." A large group of players may divide into two or more circles with a frog for each circle. Or there may be from two to five frogs in the same circle. The space in the circle may be a sea, pond, creek, or river. The players who are not frogs may be grasshoppers or animals of various sorts. Sometimes the players shout, "Frog in the sea, can't catch me."

Feeding the Elephant—Place a megaphone or cardboard funnel in a bucket or wastebasket. Each child is given ten peanuts to try to toss into the elephant's mouth